Liberalism: A Rope of Sand

A Conservative Answer
Donald G. Boys

Goodhope Press, Inc.
P. O. Box 27115
Indianapolis, IN 46227

Copyright © 1979 by Donald G. Boys

All rights reserved

No part of this book may be reproduced or transmitted in any form or by any means, electronic or mechanical, including photocopying, recording, storage in any information retrieval system, or other, without permission in writing from the publisher.

Printed in the United States of America

DEDICATION

To my wife Mary Anne; son, Michael Dale; daughters Becky, Suzan, and Tammy who put up with my working late each night; who drove for me while I worked in the back seat; who went to vacation spots alone while I worked in motel rooms. To them, I say, "God bless you for your patience and understanding."

CONTENTS

Chapter

	Introduction	7
I	Should Baby Butchers and Mercy Killers Be Imprisoned?	11
II	Should Perverts Go to Jail?	21
III	More on the Strutting Sissies	35
IV	Will the ERA Change Your Life?	49
V	Is Pornography a Victimless Crime?	61
VI	Does the State Own Your Children?	71
VII	Why Americans Flee the Public Schools	77
VIII	Must Christians Always Obey the Law?	97
IX	Should Civilized Nations Execute Killers?	109
X	Should Teachers, Policemen, and Firemen Strike?	115
XI	Are Right to Work Laws Good or Bad?	123
XII	Should Blacks Receive Special Privileges?	129
XIII	Is There a Right to Welfare?	139
XIV	Grass: To Be Walked On or Smoked?	149
XV	Do the Cultists Have Rights?	155
XVI	Our African Policy: Reasonable or Treasonable?	163
XVII	Barbs By Boys	175
	Epilogue	197

The Boys' Family
without Don & Mike

INTRODUCTION

Most sincere Americans want to take a correct position on the various controversial issues, but some don't even know what the issues are let alone what position is the "right" position. Others know what the issues are and what position to take but don't know why they should hold those views.

This treatise is to help teachers, ministers, students and all in leadership positions to identify the issues, think them through, and to help them come to a firm position that will withstand the jeers and onslaughts of the liberals - liberals who have lost their punch in recent years.

If I were a liberal, I would be embarrassed at the miserable failure of liberalism especially in the last twenty-five years. In fact, I would recognize the error of my ways, repent, and be converted and stop pulling on that "Rope of Sand"!

In this book I try to shoot the liberal out of the water as I deal with the most controversial issues facing this nation. After finishing this book, you should know the general position taken by liberals and conservatives and the reasons why you should be a conservative. Many people who were moderates 25 years ago are now forced into a conservative or "right" position. Although we have not changed our position or philosophy one iota, the "left" has gone so far left most of us find ourselves "right." If we are "right," are the liberals wrong?

Liberalism has proved itself bankrupt in every arena: political, economic, theological, and educational. I do not affirm the above simply because there is a conservative breeze turning the maple leaves of the land. We have had liberal programs sold to us as being workable and desirable and have observed that they are neither workable or desirable.

We watched America lose a war for the first time in history; a war that could have been won in less than 12 months. We were then humiliated as our forces fled that country like a philandering

Casanova hurriedly absconding through an open window with pants in hand and shoes left on the bedroom floor of a married woman. We showed little class and less courage in the whole Vietnam debacle that cost us over 50,000 American lives.

We used to be ridiculed when we talked of the domino theory relating to Communist conquests, but after the fall of North Korea, we heard the distinct clink of other dominos - Vietnam, Laos, Cambodia, etc. You don't hear much talk about dominos anymore. Most of them have been lost.

We have witnessed the dismantling of our intelligence agencies at a time when they are needed most. We are seeing FBI agents prosecuted and persecuted for defending us against terrorists while the radical activists are given "posh" jobs with the Federal government. What a topsy-turvy world: Jobs for anarchists and amnesty for draft dodgers but prosecution for FBI men who have served their country a life-time!

Americans will soon experience a reign of terrorism like that in Africa, Japan, Italy, and Germany and the credit will go to those liberals who were horrified at liberties taken by the FBI in the protection of our freedoms, but could not muster any anger at the infiltration of terrorists and KGB agents who are stumbling over each other in undermining this great republic. And only blind fools cannot see the collusion between Communist agents and cowardly death-dealing terrorists who will attempt to blast away the foundation of this nation.

We have been told that deficit spending was not bad; in fact, it was good for all nations. We were told that inflation was desired over unemployment, so we now have both. We were told the minimum wage was just and necessary and have found it is neither. The record proves that the minimum wage hurts those who need help the most - young, uneducated blacks.

We know that the minimum wage costs thousands of jobs as many positions are eliminated because businesses cannot run on fanciful theories but on a profit basis. We now know that a job is not necessarily worth a certain amount because of governmental edict. If a job is worth a dollar per hour, that is what businesses can afford to pay. I suggest that the first positions that should be eliminated are those of liberal politicians who are callously indifferent to the plight of the young, the poor, and the uneducated.

Liberal theologians have proved their bankruptcy by empty churches, seminaries, and pulpits. This has led to their inability to pay their bills that resulted in mergers. They are justifying the merger talk with the self-righteous explanation that Christ "wants all to be one". Some, in desperation, have decided to imitate the fundamentalist's methods without accepting their life-changing message; resulting in more of the same - sounding brass and tinkling cymbal.

And what shall I say concerning education that most families don't know from first-hand experience? The dropping SAT scores for the last 15 years; violence; drugs; and lack of discipline; the disaster of busing - the work of madmen and clowns; graduates who cannot read or do simple math; and finally the control of the schools by the arrogant union bosses who care more about money and power than they do kids.

Conservatives lose credibility with people when they can't refute the liberal line. Many Christian leaders walk away from a devastating encounter with liberals, muttering something about how "they didn't understand Peter, James, and John either." Leaders must have answers not excuses, especially excuses wrapped in self-righteous phrases.

Since I have been in the Indiana House of Representatives, I have been involved in numerous debates (i.e. ERA, Collective Bargaining, Abortion, etc.) with the liberals of my own party. I have also had formal debates with leading liberals at the universities. I challenged them for some answers to questions relating to perverts, pornography, reverse discrimination, etc. and never received any satisfactory answers. Well, I challenge them again on these pages for some answers.

Hopefully, **Liberalism: A Rope of Sand** will provide a valuable source of information so that leaders and students will be better prepared to give an answer when they are asked about abortion, ERA, reverse discrimination, pornography, gay rights, child abuse, licensure of church ministries and other controversial subjects. That is the purpose of this book. Most Christian conservatives get up each morning and curse the political and philosophical darkness around them. With the proper information, we can arise each day and light a candle and "burn liberals all day long".

Liberalism has proved itself to be a "Rope of Sand" and all who pull on that rope are not wise. The author hopes for two results of this effort: some conversion of liberals and more confidence by conservatives.

I

SHOULD BABY BUTCHERS AND MERCY KILLERS BE IMPRISONED?

Professor L. R. Agnew, of the UCLA School of Medicine posed this set of circumstances to his students: "Here is the family history. The father has syphilis, the mother has TB. They have already had four children. The first one is blind, the second one died. Third is deaf. The fourth has TB.

"The mother is pregnant with her fifth child. The parents are willing to have an abortion if you decide they should. What do you think?

"Most of the students decided on abortion," said Professor Agnew.

"Congratulations!" he told them. "You have just murdered Beethoven."

And there have been hundreds of thousands of Beethovens murdered by the Baby Butchers, but it must not be assumed that because Beethoven made a great contribution to the world of music his abortion would have been any more heinous than others less talented.

Inconvenience of Children

There are many motives given to justify killing the babies. Most aborting women believe that a child does not exist until birth, so abortion is not murder. That is a convenient belief when you want to do away with an innocent, helpless child. The fact is, most of these women don't want the inconvenience of children. It is difficult to lead an active social life with a baby hanging on the hip.

Others say a child should be aborted if there is danger of retardation or physical deformity. The day may come when a child, shortly after birth, must be approved or disapproved for life. The child may be denied permission to live for physical, mental, or even social reasons.

Millard Everett said in his book, **Ideals of Life,** "When public opinion is prepared for it, no child shall be admitted to the society of the living who would be certain to suffer any social handicap. For example, any physical or mental defect that would prevent marriage or would make others tolerate his company only from a sense of mercy."

Well, that sure opens a can of stinking worms. Tell me Millard, just who decides what babies live or die? Will you kill babies born blind since they would be tolerated "only from a sense of mercy"?

Most sensible people will reject the heathen, bloody suggestion that newborn babies be killed for social reasons, yet they can accept the murder of babies a few weeks after conception!

If it can be determined that the fetus inside the mother is not a child, then it can be argued that abortion is not wrong. However, if a fetus is a child, then doctors who perform abortions are truly Baby Butchers.

Life comes from God. The man produces the sperm; it unites with the egg. But God gives the life. It is known that the sperm and egg making contact will not always result in pregnancy. The reason is unknown to doctors but not to those who read the Bible.

Children Are From God

Psalms 127:3 says, *"Lo, children are an heritage of the Lord: and the fruit of the womb is His reward."* Ruth 4:3 says, *"The Lord gave her conception."* God said in Genesis 17:16, *"I will bless her, and give thee a son also of her."*

Again in Genesis 30:22 God is seen giving life, *"And God remembered Rachel, and God hearkened to her and opened her womb . . . and she conceived and bare a son."*

Now, since God gives life, is it not dangerous for man to abort that life? God will not hold mothers, doctors, nurses, and judges guiltless for this slaughter of the innocent.

The U.S. Supreme Court has upheld and even encouraged the killing of babies in its January 22, 1973 decision. You can be sure those justices who voted for abortion on demand did not open the Bible to come to their decision.

Professor Bickel of Yale University said that this question "should have been regarded beyond the bounds of judicial competency."

Bickel is correct. Of course, the Supreme Court has displayed incompetency in many areas; but that has never discouraged them from rendering incredible decisions. They see themselves as great social changers rather than adjudicators of the law.

What we need are judges with fixed terms that would require them to be re-appointed or re-elected every eight years. As it is, they sit for life in a cozy chair and are answerable to no one. They would be more sensitive to the desires of the public if they knew there would be a judgment day for them every eighth year.

Babies Not Persons

The Court decision of 1973 said that unborn babies had no right to life. Now, they have said that rapists have a right to life and killers have a right to life, but innocent babies do not! The Fourteenth Amendment to the U.S. Constitution says, "No state shall . . . deprive any person of life . . . without due process of law; nor deny to any person . . . the equal protection of the laws."

How did the "joy boys" of the Supreme Court get around the Fourteenth Amendment? Easy. They said that unborn babies were not "persons" or were "non-persons". This calls to mind the Dred Scott Decision of 1857 which held that blacks were not "persons". Slaves could be bought, sold, beaten, or even killed by the slave owner. The Fourteenth Amendment corrected that barbaric decision.

But, now the Court has said that the unborn child is not a "person" and can be killed on request of its owner (mother). We need another amendment to protect the innocent from the baby killers.

Attorney John R. Price said in his book, **America at the Crossroads,** "The Court . . . invented a new right, the 'right of privacy', which is nowhere mentioned in the Constitution. The Court found that the mother has a 'right to privacy,' but the child has no rights." Not even the right to breathe.

Dr. Billy James Hargis and Dan Lyons correctly state in their book, **Thou Shalt Not Kill ..... My Babies,** ". . . an abortionist found guilty of destroying an eagle's egg would be fined $500. The same man, killing a living embryo child, would be rewarded for his efforts by as much money or more!" What an insane world we live in.

The Court said a baby can be killed before birth but not after birth because after birth it becomes a living person with all the rights guaranteed by the Constitution. But, Dr. Thomas Johnson buried that position in his article, "Abortion: A Metaphysical Approach," that appeared in the August, 1972, issue of **The Freeman.** He asked, "Is it possible that by some magic, at the time of birth, this alleged potential being is somehow, within a matter of minutes, transformed into an actual human being?"

Dr. Johnson continued, "To rational individuals the answer is incontrovertible. Both the unborn child and the newly-born child is an actual human being and at the time of birth the child is merely moving from one required environment (aquatic) to a newly-required environment (gaseous) so that it can continue to develop into the succeeding stages of life."

Abortion on Demand

The Supreme Court Judges, after saying that a baby could be killed right up to delivery for any reason, then said, "This does not mean abortion on demand." But, that is exactly what was meant and babies are being slaughtered in stainless steel operating rooms at the rate of two million per year.

Those same mothers, doctors, nurses, and judges are no doubt horrified each Christmas season when they are reminded of King Herod and his slaughter of the babies in his attempt to destroy the Christ-child. King Herod was a nice guy compared to the Baby Butchers of today! The difference in Herod's case was that they could hear the screams of the dying children, but today it is not as soul-scarring since you can't hear an aborted baby cry - usually.

Doctor's Confession

Dr. Bernard Nathanson once headed the largest abortion mill in the western world and was quoted in **Good Housekeeping** magazine in March, 1976, saying, "I am deeply troubled by my own increasing certainty that I had in fact presided over 60,000 deaths."

Nathanson continued, "There is no longer serious doubt in my mind that human life exists within the womb from the very onset of pregnancy."

Dr. John D. Moroney, a medical doctor, wrote in the **Tampa Times** in March of 1978 saying, "Even if one should still have doubts that the fetus (at any age) is a human person the benefit of the doubt should go with life. If there is any doubt on death row that the convicted may not be guilty, society sides with the person and a stay of execution is granted. That is the least we can do for the fetus."

Amen, John!

Control of Her Body

The shallow arguments for baby killing amaze me. A mother talks of her rights to control her own body, but if she really controlled her own body she wouldn't be pregnant!

In one way, that argument is valid, and Rus Walton agrees with it in his book **One Nation-Under God.** He says, "Women should have the right to control their own lives. And in a word they do. That word is 'No!'. That's all it takes. Less than three percent of abortions are performed because of rape or incest."

So, the dear ladies become "with child" because they are without morals. By far, the greatest number of women having abortions are the promiscuous - not the poor, not welfare ladies, but relatively wealthy ladies who can't squeeze into their evening gowns, pregnant.

They crave watermelon and pickles in the middle of the night and experience nausea in the mornings because they said "yes" instead of "no" a few months earlier - but they quickly tell us it was a "meaningful relationship."

Kill The Baby

The mother-to-be, not wanting the inconvenience of carrying a child nine months and the responsibilities of caring for that child after birth, decides to kill the baby and escape the consequences of her act.

The father has no legal rights to be involved in the decision to execute the unborn child. Of course the Court has been very careful to make sure that Communists, criminals, and moral cripples have abundant rights but have denied the basic right to a child - the right to live. And they have denied the father his right to participate in a life or death decision for his child.

Dan Lyons reflects on this inconsistency as it relates to the parents of a pregnant teenager, in the May 1, 1978, issue of the **Christian Crusade Weekly.** "Lest anyone doubt the extent of the Supreme Court's hypocrisy, let him reflect on this: no minor may be admitted to a hospital in this country without the permission of his parent or guardian, no matter how small the illness or accident to be treated. That is, except the girl who wants to have an abortion!" I believe the world is run by Mongoloids!

How to Kill a Baby

After the decision has been made to kill the baby, it must be decided on how to accomplish the task. There are four ways to "get rid of the inconvenience." One way is Caesarean section abortion. This is a typical C-section until the cord is cut. Then, the child is dropped into a bucket (stainless steel and sanitized) where he is left alone to struggle, whimper and die.

Another way to abort is with salt poisoning. After 16 weeks the baby is poisoned and pickled until death. A long needle is inserted into the baby's sac and a saline poison is injected. The living child breathes in and swallows the salt while the skin is burned off by the concentrated salt. Dr. and Mrs. J.C. Willke, in a paper entitled "Life or Death," said, "It takes over an hour to slowly kill a baby by this method." About 24 hours later the mother will deliver a salt-burned, salt-poisoned baby corpse, and she'll be free. Guilty but free.

If the mother doesn't like the first two methods of killing, she may choose a D and C abortion. Here the surgeon, (who was trained in Nazi Germany) enters the uterus through the vagina with a loop knife and casually cuts the body into small pieces. There is a great amount of bleeding as the body is re-assembled on a table to make sure the womb is empty.

Have you had enough? How about one more way to get rid of the results of a "meaningful relationship"? This is the suction abortion. Here, the baby is cut to pieces as in the D and C but a powerful tube is inserted that sucks the baby into a container after tearing apart those portions of the body that were not severed by the "kindly" doctor.

Murder Mills

The UPI carried a story published in the **Indianapolis Star** in November, 1978, headed "12 women who died of infections or bleeding following abortions at state-regulated clinics." According to the article, the Illinois state officials had no knowledge of any abortion-linked deaths!

The abortion scandal was discovered by the **Sun-Times** and the Better Government Association who said their ". . . investigation uncovered numerous dangerous medical and laboratory procedures.

"These included discarding tissue samples without pathological examination, careless handling of specimens that made reports

Should Baby Butchers and Mercy Killers be Imprisoned?

meaningless and failure to use microscopes to examine specimens and samples."

The article went on to say that one of the accused Illinois doctors owns an unlicensed Indianapolis abortion mill, and he may have saved $50,000 a year on laboratory fees by throwing aborted tissue into the toilet instead of having it analyzed. That same doctor was identified as the "highest paid Medicaid doctor in the country, having been paid $792,266 in one year!" (The unlicensed abortion mill has been operating while preachers who have unlicensed pre-schools are prosecuted.)

In a nation where little children are slaughtered, no one is safe. Notice that the same crowd that yells for abortion on demand almost always demands an end to the death penalty for convicted killers. Why? Because it is cruel and unusual punishment!

Dostoyevsky said, "If God is dead, then nothing is morally wrong." But if God is not dead, and He isn't (I talked to Him this morning), then the Baby Butchers will face Him at the Judgment Bar, and maybe each one will remember his oath to humanity just before he is sentenced to eternal damnation.

Old Folks Are Next

But it doesn't stop with abortion. It goes on to euthanasia. Euthanasia means "good or easy death," but let us call it what it is - the right to kill the helpless, the innocent, the useless and all others who get in the way, and who can't fight back.

Dr. Joseph Fletcher said in his book, **To Love and To Die,** "If it is believed that the well-being of persons is the highest goal, then it follows that either suicide or mercy killing could be the right thing to do in some exigent and tragic circumstances." Fletcher's humanism bleeds out in his statement that the highest goal of man is his "well-being." There are many higher goals than that. Notice that he says that suicide or mercy killing would be the "right thing to do." We are living in a day when men call right, wrong and wrong, right.

George Paulson wrote in **Geriatrics,** March, 1973, edition, "How long shall life be preserved when there is no redeeming social value? If life has no apparent purpose, perhaps it is to the benefit of others that such lives not be salvaged." Is George saying, kill the old folks to get them out of our way so their money will be in our hands; after all, old folks are a bore and a nuisance? Someone had better tell George that if he keeps on breathing, he will be old one day.

Kill Handicapped Children

Dr. Glanville Williams in his book, **The Sanctity of Life and the Criminal Law,** boldly says he wants "humanitarian infanticide" and euthanasia for handicapped children.

Then Dr. Robert H. Williams, a professor of endocrinology wrote in the July, 1970, issue of **Northwest Medicine** that "planning to prevent overpopulation of the earth must also include euthanasia, either negative or positive." In my opinion, the overpopulation argument is nothing but a smoke screen to cover up murder.

John R. Price, in his book, **America at the Crossroads,** disproves the overpopulation myth. He wrote, "In a report to the California Legislature on population Dr. Robert L. Sassone, shows that every person in the world could live in a space the size of Texas and New Mexico, with homes, industry, and parks, and the rest of the land in the country would be sufficient to supply our food needs." That shoots down the old overpopulation argument.

Then Dr. Williams of overpopulation fame, mentioned above, wrote in the Seattle **Times** on March 7, 1973, suggesting the killing of "potential suicides" and "hopelessly criminal individuals" as well as the "terminally ill in discomfort or pain." Good job, Doc. Clean 'em all out.

Not Fashionable to Oppose Abortion

I remind you that Hitler began his murder marathon in 1939 by killing the mentally retarded. He then solved the problem of overcrowding prisons by killing the inmates and then moved on to the old peoples' homes. After killing over 400,000 helpless people, Hitler started on the Jews.

John R. Price says in his book, **America at the Crossroads,** concerning Hitler's programs, "The record shows that only three letters from German clerics were written questioning the programs . . . The churches didn't protest then, for the same reason that some American churches don't protest abortion now; it's not fashionable to oppose sin so openly." And so it isn't.

Some sincere folk, horrified at abortion and euthanasia, are confused about the moral position on withholding artificial life-supports from dying patients, but I believe a patient has a right not to "hang on" to life artificially when all hope is gone and all vital signs are absent.

A pamphlet by Mary Senander and Maureen Boisclair, entitled

"This'll Kill You," put euthanasia in proper perspective when they asked, "The question is: Are we going to say, 'I'm sorry your life is difficult. What can I do to make it better?' We are in this world to minister not murder."

Senander and Boisclair, quoted above, wrote, "A society is measured by the way it treats its young, its old, and its helpless." As you see the aborted babies dropped into buckets, you realize that as a nation, we don't measure very high.

I would remind the Baby Butchers that Proverbs 6:16,17 tells us that God hates those that "shed innocent blood." But, God does not leave us bystanders without responsibility for He said in Proverbs 21:13, *"Whoso stoppeth his ears at the cry of the poor, He also shall cry, but shall not be heard."* So, get your fingers out of your ears, the lead out of your pants, the dust off your Bible and get involved in the fight to close down abortion mills, cut off state aid for abortions and help put the Baby Butchers and Mercy Killers behind bars with the other bloody criminals.

II

SHOULD PERVERTS GO TO JAIL?

There is nothing gay about the homosexual way! Homosexuality is not normal, acceptable behavior. God created male and female and every person knows how God expected them to react to each other. Any deviation is a threat to civilization.

Whoever first called homosexuals "gay" had a twisted sense of humor. They like to present the gay life as carefree, happy, and glamorous; but surely informed homosexuals know the stark facts: Fifty percent of suicides and homicides in the large cities can be attributed to homosexuals. According to the **American Medical News,** half of the cases of syphilis in large cities can be traced to sodomites. Not very exciting is it?

Dr. Daniel Cappon, a practicing psychiatrist, says in his book, **Toward an Understanding of Homosexuality,** "homosexuality by definition is not healthy or wholesome . . . the homosexual person, at best, will be unhappier and more unfulfilled than the sexually normal person. There are emotional and physical consequences to this protracted state of mental dissatisfaction.

Homosexuals Die Younger

"At worst, the homosexual person will die younger and suffer emotional, mental, and physical illness more often than the normal person. The natural history of the homosexual person seems to be one of frigidity, impotence, broken personal relationships, psychosomatic disorders, alcoholism, paranoid psychosis and suicide . . ."

How could anyone call them gay with the above prognosis? Down through the centuries they have been called perverts. Of course, I can understand why the homosexual wants to be called gay. I don't mean to be unkind or cruel, only factual. If "homosexual" means what I think it means and "pervert" means what I think it means, then a homosexual is a pervert. Webster's Dictionary will satisfy any person honestly looking for the truth regarding terminology.

William Lester attacks the homosexual problem in his book, **Morality, Anyone?**. He says, "The community should want to prevent as far as possible her citizens from stooping to acts of homosexuality, bestiality and the like. Such acts give in to a depravity that runs counter to the virtues necessary for civilization and eats away at the strength of a nation."

Lester expresses my main position on this matter when he says, "By having laws against unnatural sex even though the laws cannot be closely enforced, the community at least inhibits the acts somewhat through fear of getting caught and at the same time prevents the depraved from boldly parading their depravity and thereby encouraging others."

No Third Sex

Militant homosexuals are pressing for their civil rights to be declared a normal third sex. However, there is no such thing. God created Adam and Eve - not Adam and Steve. But homosexuals are not freaks of nature or weird creatures of the night, living in a world of "straights." They are creatures of God made in the image of God to whom God's message comes in the same way it comes to all of us. One thing is sure: God never made a homosexual. Malcolm Boyd, a self-professed homosexual clergyman, said, "I am proud to have been created **in that way** in the image of God." Now, that's a queer statement to make, for God never made a pervert.

Boyd is either a poor theologian, or he is twisting the truth to give credence to his own untenable position. He seeks to place the responsibility for his perversion on God instead of where it really belongs: himself. But, we are living in a day when men don't want to be held accountable for their own actions, so they blame society, family, government or God. After all, if they are not responsible then they surely will not stand in the judgment some day and give an account to the God whose laws they've broken.

Ten Commandments are Absolute

Liberals tell us that we should not be too hard on people who don't agree with us. After all, there are two sides to every question. That is correct. There is the right side and the wrong side. They tell us that the right answer is whatever works best for the individual and with which the individual feels most comfortable. Rus Walton, in his book, **One Nation, Under God,** quotes Gene Ragle as saying, "that definition of rectitude, carried to the ultimate, could earn eventual sainthoods for Adolf Hitler, Joseph Stalin and Al Capone. The decisions they made worked well - for them."

God knew we needed some absolutes so He gave Moses the Ten Commandments as divine imperatives. They were not given as topics for group discussion, modification or rejection. They are commandments that you break at your peril. Jesus Christ endorsed the Ten Commandments, and He delivered the Sermon on the Mount in exactly the same way: as divine rules for human conduct. But the liberals have tried to repeal the Ten Commandments since they interfere with their personal lives.

Pigpen Morality

Malcolm Muggeridge, lifetime skeptic, editor of **Punch,** author and T.V. personality, startled his followers in England a few years ago when he announced that he had become a Christian. Muggeridge now believes, "Western culture is reverting to the nature of the beast." He says we're observing what appears to be pigpen morality. One big error today is the belief that life is supposed to be a pleasure. That is nothing but ancient hedonism. Life is rather a privilege and duty. That is one reason why suicide and euthanasia are sins. Of course, pleasure is not evil or forbidden. We get what pleasure we earn, and most pleasure comes as we serve others. By an eternal paradox, if we do our duty, it's a pleasure; if we seek pleasure, it eludes us. If we are so foolish to seek pleasure in forbidden ways, it destroys us. You may have noticed: They are no longer gay in Sodom.

There are thirty-two states that have sodomy laws and recently the U.S. Supreme Court upheld them. I want to see homosexuals helped, but I want to see homosexual activity a felony again in each state. My bill, called "Right to Decency," would have restored criminal penalties for sodomy. I have heard their screams of protest and received their hate mail. Some people have not learned that it is possible to oppose a person for what he says and does without hating him. I'm called a hater when the fact is I'm the one being hated. I don't hate anyone.

Anita Bryant Blacklisted

Anita Bryant has taken a courageous stand for morality based on her religious convictions; and she has been threatened, ridiculed, blacklisted and harassed. Remember, this has been perpetrated by intellectual snobs, queers, and the "beautiful people" of the media. These are the hypocrites who profess tolerance and yet heap coals of fire on all who don't agree with them!

Where is the American Civil Liberties Union, those Defenders of the Oppressed, the Champions of the Little People, and Paragons of Virtue? These People of Principle believe in free speech, free press, freedom of activity; and they're against blacklisting unless you are a Fundamental Christian. Why is the ACLU not demanding that Anita be heard on the talk shows and reinstated on the Orange Bowl parade telecast?

Charles Reese said in his column in the November 4, 1977, edition of the Osceola-Polk **Sentinel Star,** "When I see people who bemoan and wail the blacklisting of Communists in the 1950's but who are dead silent when Anita Bryant is being blacklisted, I conclude they are either hypocrites or Communists themselves to whom the double standard is an acceptable tactic . . . Do you think the fact that you disagree with Anita Bryant's religion automatically excommunicates her from the protection of the Constitution?"

The message is: atheists, anarchists, and abortionists have Constitutional rights, but Anita Bryant does not have in this land of the free and home of the brave.

Queer Thinking

Liberals think that just because they make an accusation of bigotry it becomes true. Anita is called a bigot and a hater because she fought to keep perverts from teaching in Christian schools. Now, that is not only queer thinking, it is stupid thinking. Maybe masturbation doesn't rot the brain but sodomy does! I am supposed to be a bigot because I believe sodomy is a despicable crime. Liberals expect you to believe the truthfulness of their statements just because they utter them. Shhhhhhh, don't wake them up, let them sleep on.

Then I'm told that many great creative men have been and are homosexuals. That is true. But great, creative men have beaten their wives, been alcoholics and have committed suicide. The only thing it proves is that creative men don't know the difference between right and wrong; or, if they do know the difference, they choose the wrong.

We are constantly reminded that there are between ten and twenty million homosexuals in America. However, numbers mean nothing when we are discussing morality. The chatter about millions of homosexuals may give them a sense of security, but it will never give them respectability. They want the Good Housekeeping Seal of Approval upon their sexual activities, but they will never get it as long as I have a vote.

Sodomy A Learned Process

At first glance, the most effective argument in defense of homosexuals is at second glance the least supportable. We are told that it is not their fault. We are told that homosexuality is inherited like small ears, a large nose or blue eyes. We are not expected to laugh when they tell us this fairy tale.

The disciples of Freud and Skinner believe it is a behavior pattern. Freud believed that homosexuality was a definite psychosis that could be cured. An article in the **Journal of American Medicine** says that homosexuality is not "innate or inborn" but an acquired or learned process. Dr. Daniel Cappon says that homosexuality is not just a mental illness but, as a moral issue, is a spiritual illness.

Dr. Thomas Chalmers of Detroit, Michigan, asserts after his investigations, that homosexuality is not mental illness, but it results from a complex set of learning factors. Of course, what can be learned can be unlearned. Ted Evans is a psychology fellow with the Neuro Psychiatric Institute of UCLA. He said in an article for the **Journal of Psychology and Theology** that there is no evidence whatever of genetic or hormonal causes for homosexuality. He said it is a socially learned process.

No Kinky Genes

Time magazine said, "The only thing most experts agree on is that homosexuality is not the result of any kinky gene or hormone predisposition . . . Male and female homosexuals do not constitute a third sex: biologically they are full men and women." So, the leaders of the homosexual movement are using fallacious reasoning when they say that homosexuality should not be condemned anymore than blackness should be condemned. My black friends do not appreciate the comparison or the reasoning.

Dr. Jerome Frank in a 1976 report on homosexuality, distributed by the National Institute of Mental Health, says that a significant number of homosexuals can become heterosexual. **Growing Up Straight,** a book published in 1969 and endorsed by the National Institute of Mental Health says, "Scientific consensus holds that homosexuality is very largely conditioned by the environment and childhood and most particularly by parental influence in the home." The book also makes a point that the propagation of the homosexual lifestyle as both glamorous and acceptable has lured many younger people from heterosexual life.

Past Civilizations Have Not Been Wrong

I want to see sodomy a felony from a moral position. I maintain that past civilizations have not been wrong in punishing sodomites. I refuse to believe that the legislatures in all fifty states have been wrong for over a hundred years in making sodomy a felony. I refuse to believe that our fathers did not know the difference between right and wrong. People with soft heads and bleeding hearts tell us that we can't legislate morality. That's a ridiculous statement. We legislate morality when we say, "thou shall not steal" or "thou shall not kill." Of course, people continue to kill and steal, but we still have laws prohibiting these crimes. Should all offenses be decriminalized? If so, we had better run to the jungle. Have you noticed that the softer society is on criminals, the more numerous and heinous the crimes committed? Our broad-mindedness has resulted in a blood bath.

Even if we agree that we cannot legislate morality, surely we can agree that the state should never legislate immorality. The state should never make something legally right that is morally wrong. Homosexuals want the Good Housekeeping Seal of Approval on their nefarious activities. I believe the state gives that approval by decriminalizing sodomy. Sin will always be with us. Laws will not eliminate it, but strong laws fairly enforced will keep many young people from entering a life of misery and hopelessness.

The taxpayers should have some rights and one right is the right to live without stumbling across immorality at every bend of the road. At least, sin can be driven underground. We have a right to walk the streets without being accosted by pimps, prostitutes and perverts. After thousands of years of civilization we have a right to expect a minimum of morality and have laws that seek to guarantee our protection. But liberals, some of them preachers, see nothing wrong with the prevailing "anything goes" atmosphere. They have demoted Christian values from the center of life to the rank of a mere competitor. And, preachers who have no moral values are as useless and unnecessary as accountants who cannot add. They are "pulling on a rope of sand." They have tried to turn Jesus Christ into an ethical example, a kind of ideal Boy Scout helping little old ladies across the Sea of Galilee.

Another Way of Loving

The preachers of permissiveness tell us that perversion is just another way of loving. It's an alternate life style. There are people who are pushing this in the schools. President Carter appointed Jean O'Leary, an admitted lesbian (**Spotlight,** August 1, 1977) to the National Commission for the Observance of International Women's Year. In her position paper called "Lesbians and the Schools" she wrote that schools should offer sex education courses, "to encourage students to explore alternative life styles including lesbianism." She calls for schools to set up a special homosexual studies program, "to foster pride in adolescent homosexuals." She wants homosexual clubs established in schools to "foster a community spirit" among the perverts.

Can you imagine that? It's already happening in San Francisco. The San Francisco school system is teaching young people that lesbianism and homosexuality are acceptable life styles. They are only alternatives to normal sexual behavior.

Homosexuals Don't Reproduce

It's incredible that we are having this discussion in our public schools and the media. Twenty-five years ago there would not have been an issue, but today it is a major debate. Why? It goes back to the fact that men don't have a rudder to guide them. Their lives have not been built upon a moral, Biblical foundation. They have not heard that certain things are right and certain things are wrong. They have been told that what consenting adults do in private is perfectly legitimate. So they say, "live and let live, after all homosexuality is a victimless crime." Oh, really? I have some news for you neighbor. It's not victimless. Homosexuals cannot reproduce. They have to recruit. Whom do you think they are going to recruit? They're after your children and mine.

I do not believe that every homosexual is a child molester. In fact, the homosexuals constantly point out that there are more incidents of heterosexual molesting than there are among the homosexuals. Of course, there are far more heterosexuals than homosexuals. What these people don't seem to understand is, we believe that if a heterosexual man molests a little girl, that also is perversion and the individual should go to jail. They are both an evil influence. But, homosexuals are recruiting, and they're recruiting the children as later testimony will prove.

How to Proselytize

I have in front of me a reproduction from an article that is called "How to Proselytize". The article tells how a pervert can recruit men to become homosexuals. The article says, "if you occasionally tire of your homosexual partner as we all do, why not try something new? Why not reach out? There are literally millions of men out there nervously awaiting your approach. All they need is a slight push or a gently coaxing shove and they're yours. How to do it? Simple. Use this handy one, two, three guide to proselytize. You can help save the world by turning men into faggots and getting a little fun out of it too." The remainder of the article contains explicit instructions on how to proselytize.

We were told that if we would remove legal prohibitions against homosexuality it would benefit society and eliminate or discourage the flaunting of their lifestyle and the odious practice of proselytizing. That is not true. The opposite has happened.

Ten years ago Leo Abse, a member of the English Parliament, sponsored legislation that made sodomy legal. However, after more than ten years of experience in England, Abse reflects on the unhappy results in the British **Spectator.** He says, "the 1500 convictions for indecency between males in public in 1975 is more than three times larger than in 1966 before the passing of the Act."

The English lawmakers thought that homosexuals would develop greater stability in their relationships and that there would not be so much bed jumping but Abse said, ". . . the extraordinary high incidence of syphilis and hepatitis among some 'gays' is an index which can only be unhappily interpreted." Now he tells us after a ten year ride down the toboggan slide of immorality.

Help For the Homosexual

The homosexual needs help. He needs to realize that his activities are sin. God said in Lev. 18:22, *"Thou shalt not lie with mankind, as with womankind: it is abomination."* No "if's," "and's" or "but's." It is sin - always. No exceptions.

The "once gay, always gay" theory is a myth that the gay activist wants us to believe. They tell us that once a person becomes a homosexual there's nothing he can do about it. But there is a way out. His name is Jesus. There is hope for the homosexual, and hope is spelled J-E-S-U-S.

Last session of the General Assembly I introduced a bill to reinstate sodomy as a crime. At the committee hearing a sex research sociologist testified against my bill saying that homosexuality has been "long known as healthy and harmless. This bill seeks to make a crime of sexual behaviors which are frequently **recommended** by clinicians for the healthy improvement and enrichment of sexual relationships."

I suggest to you that this attitude is partially responsible for young people experimenting with homosexual activity. It is presented as a desirable way of life. Will we soon hear that a sodomy chapter has been added to the Boy Scout manual and maybe a merit badge will be earned in homosexuality? People who try to make perversion as respectable as normalcy are about as unreasonable as one who compares the works of Shakespeare to a Mad magazine.

Sodomy is Rebellion

Sodomy should be a felony because of a need to provide for our self defense. Psychologist Ted R. Evans says that homosexuality is rebellion against God. I agree. God made man and woman. He developed an ingenious plan for the perpetuation of the human race.

Homosexuals are saying, "We will not co-operate with God's plan, we will rebel against God."

What if every person became a homosexual? There would not be much future for the human race. Homosexuality is a running sore on the face of our society. It is a malignancy that can destroy our civilization. I believe it is criminal not to deal with sodomy just as it would be criminal not to deal with typhoid carriers.

Homosexuality is a death blow at the family as men abandon natural relationships for unnatural relationships. It is national suicide to legalize perversion. As citizens, we have a right and responsibility to act without embarrassment to continue to define our way of life and to promote the values we hold dearest.

A state cannot be open to enemy advances if it wants to survive. A state cannot be neutral about itself just as a man cannot be open-minded, open to all opinions about whether to allow his family to be assaulted or not.

Recruiting the Young

Sodomy should be a felony because of the effect on children. A policeman said last week that a homosexual always prefers a young boy to a man. Viscount Hailsham, in his Report to the British government, called homosexuality "a proselytizing religion." It can exist only by continually recruiting new, innocent and young victims.

Sociologist Judsen T. Landis of the University in Berkely questioned 1,800 college students. More than 500 said they had been approached by homosexuals! Two thirds of them were not more than 16 years of age when approached.

Kraft-Ebing says in **Psychopathia Sexualis** that seduction of the young is something the homosexual cannot resist. If we have a law against sodomy, we will never know how many kids will be saved from the sink hole of perversion. But the law must be stiff enough to make it not worth the risk to practice sodomy.

Homosexuality should be a felony because of great practical problems. If homosexuality is to be accepted as "just another way of loving" or an alternate lifestyle, then perverts will have every right that a normal couple would have. Homosexuals would be permitted to walk down the street arm in arm. They will be in the parks on a spring day while our children witness their abnormal behavior. They will push their equal rights until they will be married and move in next door.

They will apply for permission to adopt children and have every right to do so if homosexuality is legal and proper. They will seek approval to become Big Brothers to fatherless boys as happened in Minneapolis. When a homosexual volunteered to be a Big Brother, the charitable organization knew they could not refuse him under the Minneapolis ordinance. The Big Brother officials informed the mother of the fatherless boy that the volunteer was known as a practicing homosexual. He complained to the Minneapolis Department of Civil Rights, and they agreed with him that his civil rights had been violated! The inmates have taken over the asylum.

Homosexuals in the Pulpit

Admitted homosexuals are already in the pulpits trying to tell people how to live. I'm aware that homosexuals have always been with us. But any church that ordains a pervert has forfeited its right to be called a church and should be turned into a bowling alley.

When sodomy is legal, homosexuals will strut into the classrooms and teach our kids far more than reading, math and history. They will have the students five days per week and will exert an influence on them for a lifetime.

Those of us who believe homosexuality is perversion, that pornography is as dangerous as gasoline near a fire, that prostitution is a frontal attack on the home, are told we have hang-ups. I reply that we should be proud of our hang-ups about elicit sex, cowardice, dishonesty and selfishness. We should not try to deaden our God-given sense of shame about these violations of His natural law. We are **supposed** to feel guilty when we break God's law.

We want homosexuality to once again be a crime. We want homosexuals to be pressured into seeking help and to stop living as if Christ never lived on the earth and never told men how to live. If they refuse to obey the law, they should be placed in jail after a fair trial for the good of society.

It is time for Christians and decent non-Christians to start pushing back. We have backed up too much and have been too timid because we don't want to appear unkind and cruel. Meek we must be; weak we dare not be. We have a responsibility to truth and common sense and to our children. I, for one, do not want future generations to know me as one who advocated putting degenerates in the pulpit, in the classroom and at the marriage altar!

Consenting Adults

The liberals cry that what consenting adults do in private is none of the state's business. In fact we are told that there should be complete sexual freedom. My question is, "How far will they push us if we accept that thought?" Are we to permit anything and everything? How about sex with animals and dead people?

Is there no such thing as sexual abnormality anymore? Should any and all sex acts be decriminalized? Should all kinds of perverts be permitted to work with kids as one of their civil rights? Should companies and schools start affirmative action programs to bring degenerates into the mainstream? Will the federal government mandate those affirmative action programs? Will every fifth school teacher be required to be a homosexual to keep a school from losing accredidation and any state funding?

Adults Who Love Children

The Pedophile Information Exchange of England wants to bring into the open, discussion about adults who are attracted to children. The former chairman, Keith Hose, is quoted in the August 23, 1977, issue of the **London Observer:** "I am a pedophile. I am attracted to boys from about 10, 11, and 12 years of age."

This group of queers was to have a meeting in a London hotel, but the manager canceled the meeting and left them standing in the gutter. Dr. Edward Brongersma, a Dutch Member of Parliament and lawyer, was to speak to the group and was so upset at being canceled, he stomped out of the hotel in anger in his high heels. With tears in his eyes, (making a mess of his make-up?) Dr. Brongersma told the **London Observer,** "I was very disappointed about the ban. I wanted to tell people that it is not wrong if a man wants to have a sexual relationship with a child. It can be a very beautiful thing." Now, am I a bigot because I want these child-rapers to spend 21 years in a state pen? Then so be it.

The Body Politic's December-January, 1977, issue ran a five page article by Gerald Hannon entitled, "Men Loving Boys Loving Men." Hannon tells it all relating to boy-love. He tries to gain a little respectibility by comparing the boy-lovers to C. J. Atkinson who founded the YMCA. He suggests that Atkinson was a pedophile.

This statement is absurd and, in my opinion, is character assassination as well as cowardly in that Atkinson cannot defend himself.

Boy Lovers - Great Men

The author says that the boy-lovers "will earn the affection of their associates and friends because they have lived honest and loving lives, have formed meaningful and responsible relationships." Can you believe that? The prophet Isaiah spoke of these people and this kind of generation when he said in Is. 5:20, *"Woe unto them that call evil good, and good evil."*

Hannon tells us of some boy-lovers who will "earn the esteem of their community for the work they do with boys." One is Peter, age 48, who is rich, trim and cool. He likes boys aged 12 to 14 but is experimenting with a seven-year-old boy! Peter should not be held in esteem - he should be tarred and feathered. I'll get the tar. You get the feathers.

Hannon tells of a teacher who has taught in four different schools for ten years and has had abnormal relationships with young boys in each school. He is also a Big Brother to a fatherless boy!

Claire Hoy commented on these boy-lovers in the December 22, 1977, issue of **The Toronto Sun,** "How sick can these people get, these homosexual activists who whine that society picks on them, and all they want is equality? Equality to do what? Equality to little kids, to poison our children's minds, to get into the schools and recruit kids while they're young and impressionable . . . surely toleration of this is the first stage of decadence . . . they're bloody criminals, these people." Amen, Claire!

Tom Reeves wrote in the December 24, 1977, issue of **Gay Community News** saying, "love between men and boys is often the most mutually beneficial, the least manipulative, the least transient and the most liberating."

My question again - do we permit anything? How far do we go? Do we treat the child rapers like gentlemen or "bloody criminals"?

But, friends, "you ain't heard nothing yet." Along comes Dr. Alayne Yates, a psychiatrist and pediatrician in Los Angeles. According to the May 15, 1978, edition of the **San Francisco Chronicle,** Alayne believes that kids should not only engage in sexual experimentation, but that parents should encourage them to do so! She said, "I think masturbation needs to be encouraged in children."

Sex For Children

Dr. Yates wrote **Sex Without Shame** and builds on the premise that sex problems in adults go back to early childhood restrictions regarding sex. The answer? Sex for children! She even says that brother-sister sex "is probably quite common already and relatively normal in families today." She said, "I know a 4-year-old boy who had intercourse with a 6-year-old girl and neither seemed damaged by it."

But Dr. Yates saved her best punch for the last when she said, ". . . any kind of early, pleasurable sexual experience tends to augment later sexual adjustment and enthusiasm. And father-daughter incest is frequently pleasurable." She cautions that the daughter must be very young "and therefore untouched by the religious and cultural taboos against incest." I believe psychiatrist Yates needs to see a good psychiatrist or better yet an old fashioned altar.

If we listen to the liberals and permit everyone to do his own thing and accept and approve sodomy and other sexual aberrations, then the future surely looks bad for baby doctors and good for psychiatrists.

III

MORE ON THE STRUTTING SISSIES

"Response to a Pervert"
Rep. Don Boys

Since I became your representative, I've been called or likened to the KKK, witchburners, Joe McCarthy and now a Nazi stormtrooper. I just received a letter from a man who said he fought World War II to rid the world of people like me. Throughout his letter he tried to prove he was a wit. He was half right.

The writer is a pervert. He signed his letter "a homosexual." So, he's not only a sodomite; he's a coward as well. I don't hate perverts; I just want to see them in jail away from decent, innocent people. That's what my bill to reinstate sodomy as a crime would have done. The writer said, "We have found one of three things could be bugging you."

Well, first, who is "we"? Did you and your twinky friends meet in a darkened garret to discuss me and my bill? You suggested, "you are in doubt about your own sexuality." Now this is one thing I have never considered. What is sexuality? How do you get it? How do you lose it? And when you lose it, how do you regain it? If you have it, how do you keep it? You have me scared. Maybe I should stay home tonight and worry about my sexuality.

Next you said, "You have been turned down by a homo because you're either dumb, ugly or 'sinile.' Well, I may be dumb, ugly and senile but at least I can spell 'senile.'

Then you tried to justify your perversion by saying, "Perverts have been with us since the beginning of time." May I remind you that so have warts, flat-feet and gout, but I don't want any of these afflictions even if they do go back to antiquity.

You then showed a flash of brilliance by justifying perversion because it is "nature's way of keeping the world's population in balance." Wow! You're wasting your time writing to a lowly Representative. You should be advising those in the U.N. on world problems.

You said, "You are the type of a goon who would laugh when you see someone in a wheelchair, or a blind person or call a colored person a nigger." Here, you are a little less than brilliant. Are you trying to compare the afflictions of a blind person or lame person to a pervert? And are you further saying that if I criticize you for your perversion, I would likewise criticize them? If so, you have a problem with your mind as well as your morals.

Homo, you closed your interesting letter by saying, "Here's hoping you die of cancer, you — — —." Now if you don't like me why don't you stop beating around the bush and just say it?

"Don't Behead the Messenger"
Rep. Don Boys

Recently, an admitted homosexual wrote me calling me a Nazi because of my bill to reinstate sodomy as a crime. In my weekly newspaper column, I called him a pervert. Two letters to the editor recently indicated the writers don't like the word "pervert." But, if I know the meaning of "homosexuality," and the meaning of "perversion," then a homosexual is a pervert. Some of my critics need to spend less time writing to newspapers and more time studying the dictionary.

These are the kinds of people who behead the messenger because they don't like the message. I've had overwhelming response for my position on this issue from professional men, business men, leading state politicians and ordinary citizens.

One writer to the Franklin **Daily Journal** was not very excited over my position, however. In fact, she was appalled. Now, she was not appalled at the obscene letter I received, but she was appalled at my blunt reply.

Well honey, I'm also appalled. I'm appalled at the way some folk accept perversion as being almost proper. I'm appalled at college kids bedding down together without benefit of marriage vows.

I'm appalled at women who murder their babies in abortion mills without remorse. I'm appalled at some liberals who blame society for crime rather than criminals who perpetrate the crime. I'm appalled at some judges who permit violent criminals to walk the streets to prey on innocent, helpless victims.

I'm appalled at some politicians who make decisions not on merit, but on how it will be "perceived in the district." I'm appalled at journalists who are more concerned with "getting out the column," than with writing an accurate and fair column.

I'm appalled at some preachers who tell people what they want to hear, instead of what they need to hear. I'm appalled at dead-beats who refuse to work, but expect working taxpayers to provide for them. So you see, I can be appalled as much as anyone.

It was suggested that I am not "enlightened" because I believe perversion is a blight on society. The writer professed to be enlightened because "such matters are personal." She mentions that perhaps she is "an idealist." No, she's not an idealist. She's a liberal.

She believes that whatever consenting adults do is their business. I don't. Sodomy is still a crime in Indiana until October 1. A homosexual can go to jail for many years. In my opinion, it was a tragic mistake to repeal that law.

Sodomy won't be a crime after October 1, but it will still be a sin, and our legislature can't repeal that.

Perverts will expect to teach in our public schools, work in the Boys' Clubs and act as Big Brothers. Do you believe that this is in the best interests of society? What about the best interests of the kids?

If liberals think Indiana citizens are willing to accept perversion as an "alternate lifestyle," or as "another way of loving," they have misread the opinion of the people.

But the liberals and homosexuals would like to behead me when all I'm doing is carrying the message.

Homosexuality is perversion. We will never accept it as anything else — even at the cost of our heads. And, I will not accept perversion, even at the price of an election.

June 7, 1977

THE DAILY JOURNAL
Att. Robert Reed
P.O. Box 366
Franklin, Indiana 46131

To the editor:

"Sodomy charge dropped" so reported the **Indianapolis News** on May 28, 1977. According to the story written by Paul Bird, five perverts were involved in a public act of sodomy in an eastside bar. The two women involved had removed all of their clothing and while the customers watched including vice officers, the women engaged in "intimate unnatural sex acts with two male customers." In full public view!

Well, of course the whole bunch was hauled off to jail and after a fair-fast trial they were relegated to obscure cells away from thieves, pickpockets and drunks for fear of being a corrupting influence on those inmates. No, according to the story, the Marion County prosecutor will not prosecute because "they were consenting adults."

I believe the inmates have taken over the asylum! It's bad enough for the liberals to tell us that what consenting adults do in private is all right, but now we're expected to accept perversion in public places, "even in a public park or public business."

I'm convinced our nation is in a moral tailspin as a result of liberals in the legislatures, judiciary and the media. If God does not bring judgment upon us, He will be forced to apologize to Sodom and Gomorrah, whom He destroyed.

I submitted a bill in the last session of the legislature to reinstate sodomy as a crime. It will no longer be a crime as of October 1, 1977. My bill would have called for up to eight years in prison for sodomy - public or private. However, two pastors of homosexual churches appeared in committee and testified against my bill. A sex research sociologist from Bloomington also testified against it. Concerning sodomy, he said it has been "long known as healthy and harmless . . ." He further said in his handout, "this bill seeks to make a crime of sexual behaviors, which are frequently **recommended** by clinicians for the **healthy improvement** and enrichment of sexual relationships" (emphasis mine).

My bill was killed by liberal Republicans and Democrats. After all, we don't want to upset the perverts in our state. Of course, it doesn't seem to bother the politicians about the moral climate we must live in or the effect this kind of activity has on our children. We must never infringe on the rights of the perverts, liberals, communists, pornographers and criminals. This is the day of equal rights unless you happen to be a Christian, conservative, white male, Creationist.

If you belong in that category, the legislature and the judiciary . . . can jump up and down on your rights with the hobnailed boots of blind bias and the ACLU and similar groups will turn the other way.

And what will the Christian, conservative, white male, Creationist do about this violation of his rights? What will his reaction be to public acts of sodomy? Nothing. He is too busy making a buck to write a letter to the editor. He is too involved in his church to get involved in an issue like making sodomy a crime. So he will do nothing.

I speak for myself alone; I am concerned for homosexuals. They are disturbed, unhappy, tormented people. They need help! I have tried to help some of them. However, they will never get help if they are convinced that they are normal. They are not normal and only a fool or an ignoramous says they are. I'm concerned for them, but I am more concerned for the children in this state and for the moral climate we live in. I will join other concerned members of the legislature to protect the decent people of this state from the strutting sissies who flaunt their perversion and try to get us to accept it as normal.

The legislature has repealed sodomy as a crime, but it will take a much Higher Court to repeal it from being a heinous sin.

Sincerely,

Donald Boys
State Representative

DB / mr

June 22, 1977

Mr. Randy Haymaker
The **Times**
23 East Main Street
Mooresville, Indiana 46158

Dear Mr. Haymaker:

Aristotle said "There really is . . . a natural justice . . . that is binding on all men." He agreed with Sophocles who said, "an unjust law is not a law." Cicero, a great attorney, said "true law is right reason in agreement with nature; it is a universal application unchanging and ever lasting . . ." St. Thomas Aquinas said "if on any point (a statute) is in conflict with the law of nature it at once ceases to be a law: it is a mere perversion of law."

I suggest that our preoccupation in recent years over the rights of perverts, pornographers, Communists and criminals is a perversion of law; it is national suicide to emphasize the right of law breakers over the law-abiding. It is cultural and moral suicide to attempt to make perversion acceptable and our posterity will look back and marvel at our madness.

A letter to the **Indianapolis Star** on June 20, by Attorney Martha Michaels illustrates distorted thinking on the part of the liberal crowd who appointed itself the champion of the downtrodden and the savior of the weak. However, the liberals spend half their time and money coming to the defense of the criminals and Communists and the other half of their time and money stomping on the rights of Christians and conservatives with the hobnailed boots of blind bias.

Mrs. (or is it Miss?) Michaels' letter is filled with fallacious arguments, but then you don't have to be logical and informed to be an attorney do you? She knocked Anita Bryant because she is not "an expert on homosexuals, pornography, and prostitutes." Anita never claimed to be. She doesn't have to be an expert on sex crimes to know she is against them, anymore than Michaels needs to be an expert in citrus acids to know when orange juice is rancid.

Attorney Michaels questions how appropriate it is for Anita Bryant to come to Indiana and to "campaign for or against something which does not affect her in any way." Immorality affects all in our great Republic, even if just one state is affected. It is like a man with cancer on two fingers, but he doesn't get concerned "because after all, I have ten of them."

Then I would ask Attorney Michaels if she felt the same way when President Carter interjected himself into the different states in favor of the Equal Rights Amendment? That arrogant activity by Presidents Ford and Carter even transcends our argument since it involves states' rights.

After our dear attorney lifts the pretty locks of Miss Bryant, she then goes after Reverend Lawson with her hatchet. Of course she will take his scalp in love and in tenderness (only liberals can demonstrate love and tenderness). She will expect him to demonstrate true Christian co-operation and ministerial decorum by standing still while she performs her civic duty and decapitates him.

She says that such anti-gay activity will only drive homosexuals underground. What she doesn't understand is - that is where we want them. I introduced a bill in the last session of the legislature that would have made sodomy a felony after October 1, 1977, but

More on the Strutting Sissies

my liberal friends defeated it in committee. I said at the time that if you make perversion legitimate, perverts will come out of the closets and expect to be treated like normal people. They will be teaching in our schools, acting as Big Brothers, adopting children and marrying each other!

Michaels then stated that sodomy in public would be a crime after October 1, because of other statutes. She is technically correct but, practically speaking, she is in error. She must not be familiar with the statement from the prosecutor's office that he would not prosecute sodomy if it took place "even in a public park." This was his reaction to sodomy committed in an eastside bar in view of customers and police officers as reported in the News on May 28th.

She closed her missive by saying Reverend Lawson "should consult an attorney before making public statements concerning an interpretation of the law." Of course, that would not guarantee that he would receive competent advice. I wonder if that also means that she should contact a theologian or philosopher before she makes statements on morality?

In our society, a homosexual has the right to exist. I also have the right to refuse to hire him, and I will exercise that right regardless of laws, courts, and other pressures. I am now writing legislation to give some protection to the average slob who works an average of 50 and 60 hours a week and turns over more than 40% of his total income to keep a regular salary coming to the judges, legislators, public defenders, welfare cheats, prosecuting attorneys and welfare workers. I will continue to work with other members of the General Assembly to keep the strutting sissies from tramping over thousands of years of cultural mores and biblical teaching, and to keep us from sinking into a moral Dark Age when "every man did that which was right in his own eyes."

Sincerely,

Donald Boys
State Representative

DB / ld

Boys' statement to a crowd of 8,000 in Indianapolis on October 7, 1977, featuring Anita Bryant to raise support for his Right to Decency Bill.

RIGHT TO DECENCY

Colonel Bill Travis pulled his sword and drew a line in the dirt of the church compound outside San Antonio, Texas, in 1836 as the cannon shells fell around them. About one-hundred eighty loyal Texans and Americans including Davy Crockett and Jim Bowie were fighting the War of Independence between Texas and Mexico.

General Antonio Lopez de Santa Anna was leading the siege against the Alamo with four-thousand Mexican troops. The results were never in doubt. The brave Americans were doomed. Hence the line drawn by Travis.

Travis said, "All those who will fight to the end for the cause of Texas, step over the line." Every man crossed the line except Jim Bowie who was mortally wounded. Two friends carried him over the line.

One-hundred eighty men died in the shelling or were brutally murdered by Santa Anna. All in vain? No, for "Remember the Alamo!" was the rallying cry for years after Texas won her independence.

In like manner, we are in a war. It's a war between those who believe "anything goes" and those who believe there are some limits to what a state can and should permit.

Those of us who believe that there should be moral boundries have drawn a line and we say, "No further. We draw the line here." We will take our stand on the side of decency, civilization and culture. We are saying that thousands of years of civilization have not been in vain.

We believe our legislators in all 50 states have been right for over a hundred years identifying sodomy, rape, seduction, incest, prostitution, public indecency and bigamy as felonies. We refuse to admit that our fathers did not know the difference between right and wrong.

I have written a bill that I call the "Right to Decency" bill. I'll introduce it in the next session of the General Assembly. It will restore sodomy as a felony and will increase penalties for rape, bigamy, incest, prostitution, seduction, and public indecency. If a man rapes a girl under 15, he will go to jail for life with no suspended sentence and no parole.

I have been painted as super-pious, self-righteous, bigoted, a bible thumper and full of hate. Of course, the accusers will not substantiate the charges since they are without foundation. But, then liberals are confused people. They seem to think that by

More on the Strutting Sissies

making a statement it becomes a fact.

In fact, the liberals have mounted a campaign to "hate the haters and will never see their inconsistency. They can't see because they're blind.

The liberals, who are so concerned about the rights of the homosexuals, prostitutes, rapists, et cetera, without being concerned over the rights of the vast majority of citizens, can try to convince our people and the legislature to champion their cause.

We have the same right to present the opposite view. We will try to convince the General Assembly that homosexuality is an attack on civilization and a running sore on the face of society. We will try to have sex criminals treated fair, fast and firm. But we insist that if they do the crime, they must do the time-in jail, not a country club.

The charge is made that if we limit the rights of homosexuals and prostitutes then our rights will also be taken some day. However, every law infringes on someone's rights. It is the function of government to protect the people, and we are not being protected.

I am asked, "What about consenting adults?" There are some limits even to what consenting adults may do in private. It is unlawful for consenting adults to make a suicide pact, to commit euthanasia and abortion. Ladies and gentlemen, radicals would have us accept abnormal behavior as normal. They tell us that God did not give us the Ten Commandments to live by; He only gave us Ten Suggestions! They want us to conduct our lives as if Jesus Christ never walked on earth and told us how to live. They want to live as if a Book was not written that begins, "In the beginning, God. . ."

When determining whether a law is good or bad we must consider the effects on society. I believe the "Right to Decency" is a good and necessary bill.

I am surprised and pleased that so many people have been quoting Christ in recent months. They talk of His being so forgiving, but they never imply that Christ always forgives after repentance.

We are often reminded that Christ spoke to the woman taken in adultery, and He said to her, "Neither do I condemn thee." But no one has yet finished His sentence. He told the woman, "Go and sin no more." Men don't want to hear that.

We must always be compassionate and concerned, but we must also think of our children and their future. Just how broad-minded are we expected to be? Must we tolerate everything? Don't we have a right to walk the streets without being accosted by perverts, pimps, and prostitutes? Don't we have a right to be free from the flaunters?

We are saying with this bill, "We are drawing the line . . . we have a right to decency."

October 21, 1977

Editor
THE INDIANAPOLIS NEWS
307 North Pennsylvania Avenue
Indianapolis, Indiana 46204

To The Editor:

It seems I am spending more and more time writing letters to the media who do a good story on me, or else I am correcting their errors.

Take the **Sunday Star,** for example. They reported that we had 500 people at our March for Decency to the Circle. Now, I am aware that some reporters have trouble reading; but I thought they could at least count. We stopped counting at 2100 on the Circle Saturday morning. Yet, the **Star** reported 500. The night before, there were 200 homosexual pickets at our rally with Anita Bryant; yet, the reported crowd was 800. Very interesting.

Then take UPI reporting me as saying on Friday night, "We will attack the criminal and a running sore on society." The sentence is gibberish, and, I never said we would attack the criminal. How does such a ridiculous sentence get by the editors? Many reporters take pride in their work and are accurate and unbiased, while others are sloppy and display such an obvious set of bias not seen since W. C. Fields looked into the merits of the temperance movement.

Moving right along to the **Indianapolis News** and Wade Mann. Mann makes his first mistake by not knowing that I represent Johnson County, not Indianapolis. Although it's a minor error, it shows a lazy attitude toward details.

Mann is wrong again when he says that expunging the ERA would wipe off the record of our actions on the Equal Rights Amendment. The record would still be in the House Journal, yet expunged by following the precedents in Massachusetts, Georgia and the U.S. Senate. The offensive statement would have a black line drawn around it and " expunged. by the order of the House!" written across it. However, it would still be physically on the Journal. Then Mann tries to divide our ranks by pitting the expungers against the rescinders. He further tries to place me with the crowd who believes rescinding is illegal. I have never implied that rescinding is illegal. But, if rescinding is not upheld it will obviously be wise to expunge.

Mann then tries to put words in my mouth by saying that I would never be satisfied with rescinding; I would only accept expunging, as if expunging is something holy in my mind. I suggest that he say what he wants to say clearly, accurately, and honestly, and not try to speak for me.

Obviously Mann did not research his subject. Had he done his job he would have discovered that expunging is an honorable and legitimate legal procedure. He would have found precedents in other states and would discover that **Roberts Rules of Order** recognizes its legitimacy.

Mann closed his missive by having us anti-ERA'ers singing "Oh how I wish it would go away." No, if wishing would do the job, I would wish that reporters who can't read, count, research or write would go away.

Sincerely,

Donald Boys
State Representative

DB / ld

"WHOSE OX IS GORED"
Rep. Don Boys

I'm beginning to believe that the real legitimate conflict of the church and state issue has been lost in left-wing rhetoric. Christmas programs in schools, chaplains in the military, morality taught in public schools, references to God in public life and on our coins, are alleged by irresponsible and uninformed people to be a threat to the state, and a direct violation of the United States Constitution. Intellectually speaking, my reply is poppeycock, balderdash and a generous portion of hogwash.

However, the lunatic liberals have tried to snow us by suggesting, even demanding, that God and morality have no place in public schools, parks, the military, etc. I see a disturbing trend in our nation to use the church-state issue to keep active conservative Christians from public office. Nevertheless, to my knowledge, not one editor or journalist has come to our defense. Now, maybe they don't read their own papers, or maybe they don't care.

Because of my Right to Decency bill and a rally held in Indianapolis with Anita Bryant to promote that bill, I have been attacked in the press and no one seems aghast at the radical ravings. UPI carried a story on our rally, and quoted the Reverend Jeanine C. Rae as saying the rally was, "a misuse of religion and God as a means of persecution. Now is the time for all persons to recognize and prevent the potential merger of government with church by refusing to let fundamentalist church men and women into governmental positions."

Right on, Jeanine. Make second class citizens out of fundamentalists even though America has agonized for 200 years to guarantee equal freedom for all. Would you also take our right to vote and maybe our other rights guaranteed by the Bill of Rights?

Jeanine, I can respect you and will even defend your right to hold and preach your warped views if you are consistent. Since you believe conservative church men are a threat to our Constitution, do you also believe liberal clergymen are a threat and should not be elected to public office? In other words, do you believe all clergymen should lose the right to run for office, a right that has even been extended to Communists? Will you suggest that the five liberal clergy Congressmen resign their office, or at least not be permitted to run for office again? Or, do you make an exception in this case since they are all knee-jerk liberals?

This dangerous trend is seen again in a statement made by Lola Nelson from Auburn, the Vice President of the local National Organization for Women. She is quoted in the Fort Wayne **News-Sentinal** as saying, concerning conservative church people at the Indiana IWY meeting, "Whatever happened to the separation of church and state? If the church wants to keep its tax exempt status, they'd better keep out of politics."

But Lola, the IWY meeting was not supposed to be political! It was a "coming together of all kinds of women in Indiana." Don't church women qualify? I can assure you that all kinds of women were there. I mean **all** kinds.

Furthermore, let me assure you that concerned church people have no intention of backing off when moral issues are at stake that affect their families, even if the price is the loss of tax exempt status. And my question to you, Lola, is, Would you also, to be consistent, demand that the liberal religious groups remain silent concerning recognition of Vietnam and Cuba, the Panama Canal issue, homosexuality, civil rights, ad infinitum? My, my, my, it's so difficult to be consistent, isn't it?

Article I, Section 5, of the State Constitution says, "No religious test shall be required as a qualification for any office of trust and profit." Do we still believe this, or not? When are the left-wing, right-wing and moderate editors going to attack this premise that there should be a restriction on conservative clergymen in office?

If I demanded that Congressman Drinan of Massachusetts resign from Congress because he is a left-winger, the ACLU, the newspaper people, and the TV people would be strait-jacket material. But, since conservatives are attacked, that seems to make the difference. Well, I suppose it all depends on whose ox is gored and whether it is gored on the left or right!

IV

WILL THE ERA CHANGE YOUR LIFE?

Folks, we've been conned. The ERA is not a simple Equal Rights Amendment. We might as well face it; we've been had. We have been served a generous portion of phony balony by the shrill feminists of the National Organization for Women and similar groups. Of course, they had help from assorted busy-bodies, do-gooders, lesbians, preachers, politicians, and henpecked men who were all vainly "pulling on a rope of sand."

Other women, less militant, are telling us that they need the ERA "to end oppression and slavery." These women do not use these two words "oppression" and "slavery" as hyperbolic words. They want us to believe that they are oppressed and enslaved.

These women are justified in pointing out past discrimination in labor, education and credit; but it is just that - past! If the Equal Rights Amendment becomes federal law, it will become the most dangerous and deceptive piece of legislation ever put across on the American people. It will have a damaging and disruptive influence throughout our nation.

Equal Treatment Not Good

I think it is obvious to all thinking people (that excludes many leaders in the feminist movement since those dear ladies can't think and scream at the same time) that we will never have true equality and **should not have.** It is desirable and in the best interests of our nation to treat people differently - not on the basis of color or religion but on the basis of circumstances. We should treat folk unequally but not unfairly.

Some examples are in order: I will open a door for a lady but will permit a man to open the door for himself. In some countries a woman's hand is kissed, but normal people don't kiss a man's hand; they shake it. We stand when a lady enters a room but not for a man. Civilization has come a long way baby, but the libbers want to drag us, kicking and screaming, back into the Dark Ages where unreason rules.

There are times when people are treated unequally even in religion, without it being unfair. Some airlines serve beef to Jewish passengers while the rest of us have to eat ham. I don't eat ham; yet, I don't scream about equal rights. I think it is good that the airlines respect religious beliefs.

The pro-ERA people want equal rights in every area of life. What folly! If we could not discriminate as to age, then twelve year old kids would vote. (Maybe they would do a better job than the adults who vote as per the orders of their union bosses.) A healthy thirty year old would collect social security rather than wait until he qualifies by reaching the required age. Eight year old kids could get married (and be divorced by their tenth birthday).

If we could not discriminate according to income, then low income housing would be available to people making $30,000 per year. Anyone would qualify for welfare and food stamps. (Don't they now?)

We were not asked to vote on a simple general amendment to give support to women or to solve a single problem relevant to women. (Anybody could do that.) We were asked to pass a law that will affect every person in this nation and invalidate thousands of necessary state laws.

Churches Will Lose Tax Exemption

If the ERA passes, the National Organization for Women and similar groups will appeal to the courts to challenge the constitutionality of your right to worship. On page eighteen of **NOW's Leadership Manual** they screamed, "We demand that Title VII of 1964 Civil Rights Act be amended so that religious groups no longer have legal sanctions to discriminate on basis of sex." That will wipe out all denominations who refuse to ordain women. That would be the Baptists, the Roman Catholics, the Greek Orthodox, the Jewish groups and some other groups.

Professor William Marsh, Professor of Law at Indiana University Law School, admitted this at a public hearing on January 4, 1977, when I asked him what would happen to those churches who don't ordain women under ERA. He did not hesitate. He said they would lose their tax exempt status.

Most denominations cannot exist without a tax exemption if they are to continue operating hospitals, schools and orphanages. The federal government will be in the business of telling churches what they must believe. Even those who believe in ordaining women should still get into the fight for the right to run our churches according to our own conscience and our own concept of theology.

Homosexual Marriages

Under ERA, homosexuals will be treated on an equal basis with normal people. They will teach in our schools, marry a person of the same sex, file joint tax returns, and adopt children. Professor James White of the Michigan Law School testified at the U.S. Senate Judiciary Committee saying, "Conceivably, a court would find that the State had to authorize marriage and recognize legal rights between members of the same sex."

Bruce Roeller, of the National Gay Group, said that attorneys for his organization are ready to go to court to challenge laws that discriminate against gay people.

Roeller was quoted by a New York paper as saying, "Why should we be denied a marriage license just because we choose to marry a person of the same sex? . . . If it's legal for a man to marry a woman, then it's sex discrimination to say that he cannot marry another man. The ERA bans sex discrimination of **any** kind. We will continue to appeal our cause to this higher law, and we are confident that we will win our full rights." Of course, this is exactly what pro-family critics of ERA have been saying would happen if the ERA becomes law.

Jean O'Leary, also of the National Gay Group, added, "We've been waiting for the Federal ERA to be ratified before filing some of the test cases that we have been contemplating. Lesbian and homosexual couples can be loving parents and teachers, and we want the right to adopt or teach children without discrimination based on the sex of the person we are married to."

O'Leary continued, "State and federal lawmakers have been afraid to help us in the past because of political reasons, but the courts don't have to worry about voters and politics. The ERA will open the door to full equality for gay people. Eventually, we will be able to teach children that homosexuality and lesbianism are positive, **alternative** life styles. The future looks bright for gay people." Yea, and bleak for normal people.

Women in Combat

If the ERA is ratified, and we experience another war, your daughter will register for the draft and will be drafted. She will serve with men even in combat and conceivably end up a prisoner of war. Only a fool or a Pollyanna personality would say that war is a thing of the past. The U.S. House Judiciary Committee report said, "Not only would women, including mothers, be subject to the draft, but the military would be compelled to place them in combat along side of men." Even Senator Birch Bayh, the daddy of the ERA, admitted this during a televised debate.

The Wisconsin **State Journal** for August 13, 1978, gave us a preview of life in the service for females, and remember we presently have a volunteer army: The report told of six female soldiers who were forced to live in a tent with male soldiers for a week! The women and their husbands objected, but without success.

The **Army Times** for October of 1977 reported that female soldiers stationed in Germany are suffering so many rapes that "an escort and guard service formed, and women had to have an escort even to visit the camp latrine."

The **U S News and World Report** admitted, "In some units up to 30 percent of the women are pregnant at a given time." Now, I've heard of your friendly military service but that is being too friendly.

The **Alan Stang Report** for the week of January 2, 1978, said concerning women drafted under ERA, "They want to reduce women to animals who would produce cannon fodder for the state."

Most of us believe that men should fight and win wars and protect and provide for the family. That goes along with the honeymoon. But, of course, the leading ladies in the pro-ERA camp have nothing to fear from the draft since they are far, far over the draft age.

Women Will Lose

Under a federal ERA, women will lose financially. I could go into great detail concerning divorce, alimony, dower's rights and social security. But a few examples will prove the point: Massachusetts has a state ERA. Four days after it passed, the Commissioner of Insurance announced that life and auto insurance rates for women would go up. It doesn't matter that women live longer than men and are safer drivers. Men and women must pay the same. Equality, right? Right! But women are losers, and in the name of equality.

Florida has a law giving widows a property tax break that was upheld by the U.S. Supreme Court in 1974. At trial time, a pro-ERA female lawyer joined in the case to void that law. Now, remember, ERA is supposed to help you ladies. Maybe someone needs to explain the word "help" to some ERA proponents.

More Jobs for Lawyers

ERA will not provide more jobs in the market place except for lawyers. ERA will not permit states to restrict, regulate or stop abortions. ERA will require a wife to be responsible for half of the financial support of the family. ERA will require police departments to water down or eliminate physical tests in order to put more women in uniform.

ERA will lift the protection of women in industry. Justice Felix Frankfurter said, "Only those who are indifferent to the exacting aspects of women's industrial life will have the naivete or recklessness to sum up women's whole position in a meaningless and mischievous phrase about equal rights."

The Commonwealth of Virginia showed prudence by appointing an ERA Task Force of distinguished law professors from the University of Virginia, University of Richmond, Washington and Lee University and William and Mary College. This Task Force, after careful deliberation, concluded that ERA will require Virginia to integrate the sexes in its prison system, and that the draft be applied to men and women with duty assignments, including combat, be made on sex-neutral basis. The Virginia law which requires that employers provide separate restroom facilities would be suspect under the kind of strict standard of review which ERA is likely to create. ERA's affect on rape, statutory rape and seduction could well be invalidated. The ERA was wisely rejected in the state of Virginia.

States Will Lose

Rus Walton said in his book, **One Nation Under God,** "If the ERA becomes federal law it will invalidate and pitch into the trash can another huge chunk of state's rights. Our state laws dealing with women's rights and protection would be replaced by federal statutes and on one more parade ground, we would be forced to march to the federal beat. It says so right here in the ERA, 'The Congress shall have the power.'"

Any observer of American history knows that when the states step back and surrender their power, the federal government steps forward and takes over. And, as Walton continued, "That is centralism. Whether you wrap it in striped pants, coveralls or mini skirts, centralism is the antithesis of freedom. It is a slide away from the Republic and an anathema to free individuals."

It is difficult to believe that any state legislature would be willing to give the federal government even more power to abuse. If the states keep on "giving away the store," we will soon spell it state's R-I-T-E-S.

The ERA is a stab in the back to the hundreds of thousands of women who don't want to compete on an equal basis with men. Many cannot compete because of age or lack of skills. Surely, the right to be a woman should be as sacred as the right to be treated like a man.

Unisex Restrooms

In every debate on the ERA, the pro ERA group has always brought up the possibility of unisex restrooms. Their group always giggles as if it is an impossibility. They ridicule us for even suggesting such an incredible possibility, but they are the ones who always mention it. However, they have stopped giggling since the following UPI dispatch was printed in the **Washington Post** on February 7, 1976: "The Forest Service is dropping the Men and Women signs over restrooms at the Bass Lake (California) recreation area in favor of unisex facilities. Officials said each of the 28 new restroom buildings under construction will contain cubicles with doors on them and they will be for both men and women." Surprise, Surprise, Surprise, the liberals were wrong again; but you can bet they are not repenting in sack cloth and ashes.

Another UPI dispatch in the **Salt Lake Tribune** for January 4, 1978, reported, "The 166-year-old (New York) City Hall men's room Tuesday was turned into a 'persons' room by the new administration of Mayor Edward Koch, who vowed during his election campaign to open the doors of government to everyone."

Time will prove the radicals wrong and ERA critics correct, but it will not be a cause of rejoicing for freedom-loving people.

The states are furnishing the dagger that will be slipped between the ribs of decent women by a small group of vocal feminists who will do the stabbing in the name of equality. Congressman Emanuel Celler said concerning ERA, "I refuse to allow the glad sounding ring of an easy slogan to victimize millions of women and children." But the feds are willing to sacrifice the American homes upon an altar hastily built by radical politicians and screaming feminists. They may get their way and make the ERA federal law but not without my loud protest. We still have that right - for now.

BOYS LOSES SKIRMISH WITH FEMINISTS

Rep. Don Boys

The **Indianapolis News** ran a column by Diane Frederick on January 17th headed, "Women Win Fight With Boys," but it should have said, "Boys Loses Skirmish With Feminists." The battle won't be over until the 38th state has ratified the ERA, and a decision has finally been made regarding the possibility of a State's rescinding efforts.

The article by Frederick did not deal with the committee meeting that rejected my expunge resolution, but it was a diatribe against me and my conservative and moral philosophy. Liberals have had a paranoid reaction to conservatives for many years, but a conservative who also takes a moral position turns the radicals into straight-jacket material. Frederick was obviously "struggling with her straps" throughout her column.

The columnist said Boys is, "a master at mustering up old myths to impose his moral views on Hoosiers by the State Legislature." What myths do you have in mind; like, perversion being an attack on society? Don't I have as much right to promote the majority views of my constituents as the promoters of permissiveness have in pitching their radical, "anything goes" philosophy? Would you liberals deny me that constitutional right? If so, you prove once again that liberals are sanctimonious hypocrites.

Then Frederick had trouble with the facts. She tried to put words in my mouth saying that, "The ERA would have men and women sharing Porta-Potties on the battlefield." Her column was shaky from the start since she was dealing with a person rather than a principle, so she tried to "punch it up" with a little humor. She failed.

She neglected to mention that I challenged the committee members, the press, other legislators and pro-ERA witnesses to really deal with the ERA issues. I called for a separation of emotion from fact. I again challenge Frederick to deal with my basic objections to the ERA.

Informed people know that under ERA, women will be drafted and fight in the next war. If you're for women getting their arms, legs and heads blown off on an equal basis with men, then I understand your support for ERA. However, if not, how do you justify being for such a cruel law that will kill women and place others in POW camps? Now, shallow people will answer this charge by saying, "there will be no more wars," "Congress can draft women now," "wars will be fought with missiles, not guns;" or "America wouldn't **really** put women in combat." Of course, if ERA becomes law, there will be no choice but to put them on the front lines with men.

If the National Organization for Women and other ERA groups have their way, all church denominations who don't ordain women will lose their tax exempt status. Do you pro-ERA'ers really want that, with the subsequent results: the closing of the schools, hospitals, and orphanages associated with their churches? If you don't want that to happen, or don't want to see the government interjecting itself into religion, then how do you answer this charge?

Do you also want to see physical requirements watered down for police and fire departments to provide for sex integrated units? Do you want state laws scrapped that assure husbands the right to establish the domiciles of their families? Do you believe a family should be forced to pay social security tax on an assumed income of a non-working wife? Do you want to void state laws that provide a property tax break for widows? Do you want a man to be legally free of providing for his family, thus pushing middle-aged women into the work force? Do you want to wreak havoc in athletic contests with third string boys going out for and making first string girls teams?

Do you want to see the special laws protecting women in industry struck down? Do you want to see two homosexuals treated as a normal couple with all the rights of a normal family? If you want to see these results, why not say so, or answer the charges rather than dancing all around them, and coming up with the sophomoric statement, "I'm for equal rights."? Every reasonable person is for equal rights, but not for the ERA.

The National Organization for Women has said that the ERA will be "a giant step for womankind" and they are right, but it is a big step backward. I'm waiting for a reply from ERA proponents, Frederick and pro-ERA legislators, but I won't hold my breath because purple is not my favorite color.

V

IS PORNOGRAPHY A VICTIMLESS CRIME?

The dam has burst and our homes are being flooded with a deluge of smut from television, newspapers, movies, and magazines. Liberals tell us that it's impossible to pass strong, anti-pornography laws that can be enforced because of freedom of the press. They say that people have a "right" to wallow in filth. Isn't it amazing that we can, and do, pass strong local laws regarding loud mufflers on cars and restrict highway bill boards and yet are helpless when it comes to moral filth?

We can even tell people in some communities that they must have concrete driveways. We can pass laws that regulate our lives, that infringe on our rights, but yet we cannot seem to pass laws that will drive the pornographers out of business!

Moral Pollution

Many people are concerned over pollution of our streams and air but cannot manage any indignation over moral pollution that thrives around us. It is impossible to live in a "clean" environment. We walk into a store and see nude magazines in front of us. We drive to church and see outdoor movie marquees advertising X-rated movies. Our kids are shown dirty movies in school and teachers expose them to dirty four-letter words. Full page newspaper ads are explicit in revealing what will be shown on the silver screen.

God is blasphemed in our homes via television. Incest, adultry, and perversion are presented as very common, and if not normal, then at least acceptable behavior; moreover, the liberals assure us that pornography is harmless and could be helpful! At least, there are no victims so we should not get "uptight" about it. However, many of us believe pornography is indicative of national decadence and personal immorality. Many times pornography acts as an inducement to rape and other crimes of violence; consequently, the heavy hand of the law should come down hard on those who produce it, distribute it and sell it.

Now, I am aware that you cannot pass a law and immediately solve all the problems whether it be pornography, patty parlors or prostitution. But, sin can be driven underground. We should be permitted to live our lives without stumbling across immorality at every bend of the road.

Christians Have Rights

Christians and conservatives have at least as many rights as the Communists, criminals and moral cripples. I am weary of the undue emphasis upon the felon's rights rather than on the rights of the people who pay their bills, work hard, pay taxes, fight wars and generally are a benefit to society rather than a hindrance.

Those people who believe that anything goes and that there should be no restrictions on pornography, usually point to the President's Commission on Obscenity and Pornography as their authority. What they do not say or know is that the President rejected the Commission's report!

The Commission ridiculed the proposition that there is a relationship between pornography and sex crimes among adults or teen-agers. In fact, the **Report of the President's Commission on Obscenity and Pornography** said, "that exposure of children to sexual materials may not only do no harm (sic) but may, in certain instances, actually facilitate much needed communication between parent and child over sexual matters." So, according to that "Blue-Ribbon" Commission, pornography can be beneficial to youth!

However, there is a slight stirring in the camp of the professionals relating to pornography. The American Psychological Association met recently in Toronto for their annual convention and heard empirical evidence that there **is** a relationship between pornography and aggression!

One paper was presented by Edward Donnerstein and John Hallam of Iowa State University alleging the above while psychologist Robert A. Baron of Purdue reached the same conclusion independently.

Many conservatives rejected the President's Commission on Obscenity and Pornography when it was released to the press. The conclusions of the psychologists at Iowa State and Purdue simply confirm the position taken by conservatives at that time.

Our position is Bible-based as recorded in Philippians 4:8, *"Finally brethren, whatsoever things are true, whatsoever things are honest, whatsoever things are just, whatsoever things are pure, whatsoever things are lovely, whatsoever things are of good report; if there be any virtue, . . . think on these things."*

President Speaks

For those who believe the Bible to be the Word of God and a reliable guide for our daily lives, that verse should settle the smut problem. However, President Nixon did not reject the Commission's report because of Bible convictions; common sense was sufficient.

President Nixon said, on Oct. 24, 1970, after receiving the report on obscenity and pornography, "I have evaluated that report and categorically reject its morally bankrupt conclusions and major recommendations. This commission has performed a disservice and I totally reject its report!" Wham!

The pro-porn people did not tell you that by vote of 60-5, the U.S. Senate rejected the report. They also did not tell you that the commission repressed it's own research and was not even honest in its final report.

They didn't tell you about the Davis-Braucht research that said, "In case of sexual deviance, positive relationships between amount of exposure to pornography and deviance were found for all age of exposure subgroups." That was not reported. The liberals, who believe that anything goes and that there should be no restrictions on what people sell or read, want us to believe that pornography is victimless. They tell us that there are no proven harmful effects from reading literary garbage. However, the President said concerning this: "Centuries of civilization and 10 minutes of common sense tell us otherwise."

Porn Causes Violence

Another commission, the Mosher-Katz Research Commission, said, "The data clearly supports the proposition that aggression against women increases when that aggression is instrumental to securing sexual stimulation through pornography." This was not reported by the President's Commission. They did not want you to know that many rape and child molesting cases are triggered by hard core pornography.

Five more commission studies showed definite evidence of aggression arousal in subjects who were first aroused by erotic sexual stimuli. That was not reported. Also not mentioned was the fact that over 250 psychiatrists and psychologists reported cases in which they found a direct link between involvement with pornography and a sex crime. Isn't it strange that a commission that was formed to give us solid information on pornography decided not to release this information?

Sex Criminals Read Porn

Many police officers will tell you of savage sex criminals that had rooms full of pornography; yet, the liberals would have us believe that pornography produces no adverse effects. Most people will admit that great works of literature have a beneficial effect; sensible people realize the opposite is also true - corrupt literature has a deteriorating and corrupting effect.

Pornography usually takes four or five different forms. One form is incest. In pornographic books and magazines, incest is presented and even encouraged by showing sexual intercourse between members of a family.

Sodomy is also vividly presented by photographs of nude men in positions of sexual arousal and stories about their sexual encounters.

Sex With Animals

Child molestation is another form of pornography which portrays dirty old men approaching innocent kids to satisfy their animal desires. Bestiality, as defined in many lawbooks, is copulation between humans and animals. This also is described and photographed. While the average American is not aware of such depravity, sex with animals is fairly common among the degenerates who read the above described filth.

There are other forms of pornography that take extreme and incredible avenues of approach to sexual stimuli. Many citizens are unaware of the fact that there are twisted men who get their "jollies" by being beaten with a whip by women wearing black boots. Some demented individuals are sexually aroused by burning women with cigarettes and putting brands on them. Sticking pins in various parts of the body and mutilating sexual parts of the body are fairly common. Still, liberals tell us that pornography is a victimless crime; however, they haven't asked the victims their opinions.

Pornography Not Victimless

Dr. Ernest Van Den Haag, lecturer in sociology and psychology and a practicing psychoanalyst says, "Pornography reduces or removes the empathy and mutual identification which restrains us from treating each other as objects of means. It excludes love, affection and any human relationship - while it makes sadistic acts possible and even inviting." Dr. Van Den Haag believes that pornography does affect the reader. In fact, he says pornography invites sadistic acts.

Dr. Melvin Anchell, a practicing psychiatrist said: "In adults, even sexually mature ones, pornography has a sexually regressive affect. It encourages sexual behavior characteristic of perverts." What did he say? Pornography encourages sexual behavior characteristic of perverts. However, we're told by people with "soft heads" and "bleeding hearts" that pornography is a victimless crime.

Children in Porn Magazines

A fairly new kind of pornography pictures children in sexual poses. The "kid porn peddlers" use children to sexually arouse warped, twisted adults. A magazine called **Lollitots** shows pornographic pictures of girls age 8 to 14. **Moppets** is a magazine that is illustrated with photographs of children 3 to 12 in obvious sexual poses. There is also a film that shows an alleged father engaging in bizarre sexual practices with his four year old daughter!

Robin Lloyd authored a book called, **For Money or Love: Boy Prostitution in America.** Lloyd said there are at least 264 different boy and girl porn magazines being sold in adult bookstores nationwide. These are not cheaply made books and magazines since they sell for more than seven dollars each.

Sex Clubs

Lloyd tells about clubs that have been formed. One, in Southern California that claims 2,500 members, is made up of parents who have incestuous relationships with their children. They memorialize this relationship in photographs and movies which they exchange with others who belong to the club or other groups advocating similar activity. Thomas Jefferson did not have that in mind when he wrote the First Amendment.

This club in Southern California, that specializes in parents who have incestuous relationships with their children and who put it on film, has a slogan: "Sex by Eight or It's Too Late." I think the death penalty is too good for scum like that.

Many people, who have been sheltered and uninformed, do not believe incest is so prevalent in this nation. They find it difficult to believe that there are hundreds of thousands of parents who assault their own children. However, the most recent studies indicate that over 100,000 children are sexually abused each year. Men and women without the new birth experience can sink lower than animals, but they can rise out of their degradation once they have trusted Christ as Saviour.

It would seem we have become a nation that does not know the difference between right and wrong; or if we know the difference, we do not have the moral courage to choose the right way. The fuzzy liberal tells us that right or wrong depends on the situation. In other words, adultery is not **always** wrong, thievery is not **always** wrong. Murder, while not to be encouraged, is not **always** wrong. Cheating, lying and swearing, all are wrong only if the situation is right!

Arnold Toynbee correctly commented on this philosophy in his **Study of History** when he said, "so far there has been no known human society in which the distinction between right and wrong, and the obligation to do right, have been denied."

Little Courage and Less Class

We Christians have been pushed back far enough. We have been too meek, too quiet and too patient with those who tell us that prostitutes, pimps and pornographers are not villains, and that we must be careful not to bruise their Constitutional rights. We have shown little courage and less class in our opposition to the forces of evil that are degrading our cities, demoralizing our citizens and damning our children.

And when some broad-minded politician (you know he is broad-minded because you can hear the wind whistling between his ears), talks of pornography being a victimless crime, he should be answered with a loud horse laugh - done with class, of course.

We will never remove all the pornography from the book stores and newsstands, but we can get some removed. We can remove it from many stores and, moreover, at least force the purveyors of porn to hide it from the eyes of decent people and their children. I want my children sheltered from such filth as long as possible.

Is Pornography a Victimless Crime?

What is pornography? I don't know, but I do know it when I see it; and I see it in "good" stores all the time. When you realize the moral environment our children must grow up in, by comparison, Sodom and Gomorrah must have resembled a Trappist Monastery.

July 14, 1978

Editor
The **Indianapolis Star**
307 North Pennsylvania Street
Indianapolis, Indiana 46204

To the Editor of the **Star:**

I read with interest Noel Rubinton's story in the July 2 issue of the **Indianapolis Star** concerning the controversy in Warsaw, Indiana, relating to the school board and their banning of three objectionable books. It called to mind the banning of a pro-Creation text on the state approved list by Judge Dugan, but no one got upset about academic freedom, First Amendment protection and rights of students to be taught Creation along with the farce of evolution. (ACLU and other radicals, where were you when we needed you?) Isn't it strange how selective the liberals are as to the objects of their horror? Banning the Creation text was good, but the banning in Warsaw is bad! In other words, ban God, but don't ban garbage. "Consistency, thou art a jewel."

I also noticed the biased headings: "School Teacher Fired for Supporting Textbooks" and "Battle Brewing in Warsaw Over Book Banning, Burning." Wonder why the **Star** did not use other headings like, "Teacher Fired for Promoting Pornography," or "School Board Takes Stand Against Literary Garbage"?

It's the same old story: any time there is an attempt to lift the standard of morality; raise the quality of education; promote Americanism, free enterprise, and decency, the liberal crowd raises the old ruse, "It is like Nazism when Hitler burned the books he didn't like."

Comparing the Warsaw issue to Nazism is as irresponsible as the following: Hitler built a good road system in Germany. America has a good road system. Ergo! Nazism flourishes in America!

One question posed in the article was, "Is there a place for profane language in public school books?" Of course, the fact that the question is asked is indicative of the degree of decadence in our society. There are still hundreds of thousands of homes where vile speech is not permitted either because of religious training or as a matter or civility and culture. We also don't eat whipped potatoes with our fingers or scratch ourselves in public.

The second question was, "Does the removal and banning of certain books from the classroom constitute a violation of First Amendment rights of students and teachers?" The First Amendment does not give a teacher the right to corrupt the pliable minds of children, nor does it give kids the right to read pornography. A teacher does not have unqualified freedom. She cannot advocate the overthrow of this nation; nor teach that two and two are six "under certain circumstances." She also cannot teach that Jesus Christ came to bring personal salvation to all who would accept it. The liberal crowd will go to any extremes to provide her the freedom to teach filth but not faith while others would say "she should teach faith but not filth."

William Chapel, school board member, succinctly stated the problem when he said, "The bottom line is: who will control the minds of the students: parents and the citizens of the community, or some external force?" Chapel was right. The local school board is responsible to reflect the desires, standards, and policies of local citizens and not the preachers of permissiveness who say, "Anything goes."

The fired teacher said of the book, **Go Ask Alice:** "I think it is good literature . . . It's realistic." Realistic it is, good literature it isn't. What is missing in a teacher who can't see pornography in a book that uses foul, four-letter words and describes immoral acts in vivid detail?

Many teachers think when they are given a classroom of students, they become "the master of the ship," answerable to no one. They act like "a dictator of a Banana Republic," and they are usually supported by the radical union bosses of the Teachers' Association. They need to understand that they work for the citizens of that school district and will give an account to them.

I'm weary of arrogant teachers who think they can teach with impunity any weird subjects from witchcraft to wine-making, whether the taxpayers like it or not. I am weary of their cry of academic freedom when they are told, "vulgarity in the classroom will not be tolerated." I am weary of their breast-beating and copious tears as they tell us how much they sacrifice for the good of children. I'm weary of their whining about their low salaries when they work nine months a year and chose of their own volition to go into teaching. I am weary of their spineless acceptance of everything their union bosses say. I'm weary of seeing them walking picket lines in disobedience to state law and hearing their self-righteous justification for these illegal and immoral acts.

It's about time all school boards tell teachers they will be held accountable for quality education in each class and that they must follow the guidelines as set forth by the board. If they don't like it, let them get another job where they will not retard, corrupt and confuse young minds.

It is unfortunate that this one incident is making the news while there are thousands of competent, dedicated teachers who are never heard from. They keep on doing the quality job they have been doing for years and these good teachers don't have any trouble recognizing pornography when they see it. I say, "Raise the pay of the good teachers, and 'pink slip' the rest."

The action of the Warsaw School Board is a welcomed fresh breeze in the prevailing atmosphere where employees tell employers what they will and will not do. Maybe this school board action in Warsaw is an indication of a return to sanity.

Sincerely,

Donald Boys
State Representative

DB / mr

VI

DOES THE STATE OWN YOUR CHILDREN?

The state wants to control the children from infancy into the public school system where it already has most of them. The liberals have been blunt about what they want to do. They have not tried to keep it a secret. They want to get the kids out of the homes, away from the parents. They have made it clear in numerous articles, studies and books they have written. For example, the White House Conference on Children said in the report to the president, "Day care is a powerful institution . A day care program that ministers to a child from 6 months to 6 years has over 8,000 hours to teach him values, fears, beliefs and behaviors." My question is: "whose values, whose fears, whose beliefs and whose behaviors?" Not yours or mine. Not those defined in the Scriptures. Evidently it's those of the federal bureaucrats.

The Joint Commission on Mental Health of Children defined morals for us. The report said, "Moral behavior might be defined as behavior which conforms to those standards which society establishes as being good or right, for which the group administers disapproval or punishment if transgressions appear." Now I have news for someone. I don't trust the behavior and the moral standards that have been established by society. Society will tell you, "Whatever turns you on is all right. As long as you don't hurt anyone else, it's perfectly all right to do what you want."

Bible Obsolete

We have seen a generation of young people grow up with this kind of philosophy, and they are people who have no foundation. They have no rudder in their existence. The Bible is obsolete according to them, and they would rather use a less demanding standard to give a minimum of direction to their lives. If kids don't have a reliable rudder to keep them straight, they will waver to and fro without any direction in life.

It's no wonder that we have over a million young people that run away from home every year. They have grown up without hearing the difference between right and wrong. They have no moral absolutes. Their philosophy is, "Do whatever feels good, whatever turns you on." That philosophy is as ridiculous as getting on a ship without a rudder and expecting to steer that ship into a safe port. Without a rudder, it is impossible. I maintain that the Bible is the only reliable rudder to keep men, women or young people straight. It is ridiculous to trust society to establish the moral code for people.

Parent's Rights Re-examined

They said, concerning parents, in the White House report, "We recommend that laws dealing with rights of parents be re-examined and changed where they infringe on the rights of children . . . amendments should re-enforce the primacy of the rights of the child."

Then they admitted their reason for wanting federally-funded day care. They said, "The primary reason for demanding day care is the liberation of women." So they want to get the mothers out of the home. At least they were honest - indiscreet but honest. They want to have the mothers out doing their own thing while the kids are doing their own thing in the day care.

A leading feminist, Kate Millett, in **Sexual Politics,** calls for an end to "present chattel status" of minors and the abolition of the family structure calling for the "collective professionalization of the care of the young." That is a most ominous statement - "collective professionalization of the care of the young." Then Kate says, "Marriage might generally be replaced by voluntary association if such is desired." I have a better suggestion. Instead of replacing marriage, let's replace Kate Millett.

Children's Rights

Dr. Richard Farson is one of the most blatant preachers of self determination of children. Farson is chairman of the Board of the Western Behavioral Sciences Institute and author of **Birthrights.** In this book he said, "Self determination is at the heart of children's liberation. It is, in fact, the only issue, a definition of the entire concept."

Farson said, "children would, for example, have the right to exercise self-determination in decisions about eating, sleeping, playing, listening, reading, washing and dressing. They would have the right to choose their associates, the opportunity to decide what life goals they wish to pursue, and the freedom to engage in whatever activities are permissable for adults."

That is one of the most outrageous statements I have ever read. Can you imagine giving children the authority to make their own decisions about what time they are going to bed and what they're going to eat? My kids would never go to bed and never eat beets if that happened. According to Farson, they should be permitted to listen to whatever music and watch whatever television they want and even make decisions as to washing and dressing. Now I don't know about your children, but we have to tell our small children when to take a bath. But, maybe children of liberals gleefully take their baths without being told to do so.

Parents Can't Be Trusted

Some Child Development people tell us that children have the same rights and privileges that adults have. Intellectually speaking, that is balderdash, poppycock and a generous portion of hogwash.

But Farson continues, "The decisions about a child's home environment should not belong to his parents alone. The child must have some right to choose also, and if he's too young to choose, his rights must be protected by having an advocate acting in his behalf . . . The child cannot avoid deriving his genetic make-up from his parents but he should have the opportunity, if he chooses to avoid their daily influence. He must be provided with the alternatives to his parents' home environment." Did you ever read such an asinine statement as that?

Then, Dr. Farson makes a statement that makes us conservatives reach for our muskets when he says that children are "compelled to learn the most outrageous, mythical and superstitious doctrines, and dogma that will incapacitate, threaten, and fill them with guilt for the rest of their lives." Could he mean doctrines of sin, judgment and hell? Frankly, friends, Farson is a fool.

Dr. Reginald Laurie told a Congressional Subcommittee, "There is a serious thinking among some of the future-oriented child development research people that maybe we can't trust the family alone to prepare young children for this kind of world which is emerging." Evidently Dr. Laurie believes that the federal government, state government, child advocates, and HEW are trustworthy and better prepared to train children than parents. I have a suspicion that parents probably love their children much more than the bureaucrats do, and that they know what's better for them than the bureaucrats do.

Child Abuse as an Excuse

Some do-gooders use the heinous crime of child abuse as an excuse to intrude into the homes and usurp the legitimate authority of parents.

Many of these people are genuinely interested in helping abused children, but most of them are only capable of identifying the problem. They can't provide the answers to child abuse.

Dr. James W. Prescott wrote a paper entitled: "Child Abuse in America: Slaughter of the Innocents." He did an excellent job of presenting the problem, but he was very superficial, amateurish, and dangerous in his conclusions. Prescott praises the Swedish law that prohibits a parent from striking his child. He asks, "Will America have to wait 100 years for similar legislation?" I do hope so. A parent has no right to torture and abuse his children, but he has the right and responsibility to spank them to help mold their character. If a parent does not break a child's will before four years of age, that child will break his parent's heart before he is 14 years of age.

Prescott then berates the U.S. Supreme Court for refusing to permit federal funds for abortions thereby forcing undesired babies into the world. He portrays those women as having unwanted babies who will grow up to be social problems and will be abused. What is Prescott's answer? He prefers to have the unwanted babies slaughtered in the womb in stainless steel operating rooms. After all, you can't hear an aborted baby cry. Yet, Prescott can not see his incredibly inconsistent position of advocating the slaughter of unborn babies to keep them from becoming abused children!

Spooked By Spock

According to Dr. Prescott your children will become child abusers if you spank them and teach them that pre-marital sex is wrong! Then Prescott compares the Green Berets in Vietnam to the war resisters. He said that surveys show that Green Berets grew up in homes where they were spanked and taught that pre-marital sex was wrong. They believed that masturbation was a sign of weakness and was a blow at their manliness. The draft dodgers grew up without punishment and no sexual restraints in the home. So, the moral is: If you spank your kids and teach them Bible morals, they will grow up to be loyal, brave, patriotic, Americans instead of limpwristed, draft dodging, strutting sissies.

We have seen a generation grow up without discipline in homes where the parents were spooked by Spock 25 years ago. Those kids, now grown, change bed partners almost as often as they change their socks; but, of course, each time it is a "meaningful relationship." This new morality is nothing more than the old immorality, without shame.

Many parents, like Eli of old, reprove their children but don't restrain them. There is a world of difference. Corporal punishment is as much a part of rearing a child as feeding him proper food. Too many parents are so busy training their pet poodle, they don't have time to train their kids.

God Speaks

For those who think God has not died nor even been sick, the following verses from Proverbs will settle the "punish or not punish" question:

"He that spareth his rod hateth his son: but he that loveth him chasteneth him betimes." (Proverbs 13:24)

"Chasten thy son while there is hope, and let not thy soul spare for his crying." (Proverbs 19:18)

"Withhold not correction from the child: for if thou beatest him with the rod, he shall not die." (Proverbs 23:13)

"Correct thy son, and he shall give thee rest; yea, he shall give delight unto thy soul." (Proverbs 29:17)

These verses are strong enough to hairlip the devil and send shock waves through the child development and child abuse Think Tanks where they spend millions of dollars of tax exempt foundation money to devise ways to take kids from "barbarians" who believe and follow the above principles.

The professional do-gooders who think they know how to rear children and want them reared without punishment had better bring help when they come to take my kids - "help" as in a division of U.S. Marines. And they had better be armed with something more powerful than Dr. Prescott's little paper, "Child Abuse: Slaughter of the Innocents."

The Final Say

It is my right, privilege and responsibility to train and mold my children. I teach my children to be honest, to be decent, to love their country, respect its laws, to appreciate its police officers, to try to excell in everything they do, to be kind and gracious, to go to a Bible preaching church and obey the Bible as the very Word of God. I will have the final say in my children's training, and I will give an account to God, not to the state or the federal government as to how I handle their training. Proverbs 5:3 says, *"My son, hear the instruction of thy father and forsake not the law of thy mother."*

I will never permit an agent of the state or federal government to teach, dominate, impress, control and warp my children. We must be careful about child advocates and welfare planners who would make the state the guardian of the children. I remind you that whoever controls the children will control the future, and I don't trust the impersonal state.

A child needs to be loved, but the state cannot love. He needs to be caressed but the state only crushes. The state cannot wipe away the tears nor dispel the midnight fears. The state cannot instill self-respect, courage, pride in a job well-done, appreciation or kindness in children. Experience has proved that government fouls up everything it touches when it abdicates its legitimate role as protector and tries to become a parent. I suggest, no, I demand that the state carry out its legitimate business and stay out of our homes.

VII

WHY AMERICANS FLEE THE PUBLIC SCHOOLS

Newspaper headlines seem to scream at us almost weekly: "SAT Scores Down Again." "Why Johnny Still Can't Read." "A Drive to Make High-School Diplomas Mean Something." "Police Patrol Schools." And, "Drugs Rampant in Public Schools."

Dr. Howard L. Hurwitz, author of 11 books, including eight highschool text books told the **National Enquirer,** "The public schools in the United States are experiencing a decline unprecedented in the annals of education anywhere in the world. I believe American education is at the lowest point in history - it's never been worse . . . I would say approximately one-third of our students are functional illiterates - even after going through school and receiving diplomas." Wow! The good doctor hit the Sacred Cow (Public School System) right between the eyes with a sledge hammer.

Public Education - Sacred Cow

But, let's take another swing at the Sacred Cow. On February 2, 1972, the Federal Government made public the results of a study entitled, "National Assessment of Education Progress." They discovered the "progress" was in the wrong direction. The researchers interviewed 86,000 children ages 9, 13, and 17 in 2,500 schools in various sections of the country. They also spoke to 8,000 young adults. Dr. Henry Slotnik, author of the 150 page report said, "Only 4 or 5 people in the whole assessment had a really good command of the English language." Only 4 or 5 out of 86,000!

That explains why UCLA says that 50 percent of freshmen students must take "bonehead" English!

Counterfeit Diplomas

The June 21, 1976, issue of the **U S News and World Report** reported on the condition of our schools with an article headed: "A Drive to Make High-School Diplomas Mean Something." The report said, "At commencement ceremonies this year, untold thousands of U.S. high school graduates are walking off with diplomas that are virtually counterfeit. After 12 years of schooling, they have not been taught minimum skills in reading, speaking, writing and mathematics." Well, well, counterfeit diplomas from state approved schools!

As these horror stories unfold, thousands of children pick up their Walt Disney lunch boxes and flee the Public School system; and can you blame them?

There are 43 million students being exposed to 2.1 million teachers in 43,600 schools operated by 16,200 school districts. The number of students in these public schools has declined by 2 million since 1972. However, the cost has increased 50%! So it seems we are paying more and more but receiving less and less. The liberals believe that the answer to most problems is more federal (taxpayer) funds. They believe "more" is always better, but sensible people know "more" usually means "worse" as it relates to education.

The schools should at least be teaching students the basics of education so that a good, solid foundation will exist on which to build a reasonably successful life. However, the foundation has been crumbling in recent years.

Tragic News

The **New York Times** reported some tragic news on May 20, 1970: "Half of the nation's adults may lack the literacy necessary to master such day-to-day reading matter as driving manuals, newspapers, and job applications, according to a study just published at Harvard University."

The **Times** continued: "This strong suggestion, advanced by David Harmon, an Israeli adult education expert now at Harvard, was supported today by officials of the United States Office of Education."

Karl Shaprio, poet and university professor, spoke to the California Library Association concerning students in the better universities. "Their illiteracy is staggering . . . I use illiteracy in the proper sense: the inability to read and write . . . As far as I can tell, the high school has now reached the level of the grade school; the college is at high school level." Thousands of parents just phoned the local Christian school for applications.

Why Kids Can't Read

The New York **Time** Magazine reported on November 3, 1968, "The public school system of New York City is on the brink of collapse . . . The origin of the crisis is simple. The public schools have not been able to teach most black children to read and write and to add and subtract competently. Ghetto schools have therefore become little more than custodial institutions for keeping the children off the streets." Please note that those schools are fully accredited with state certified teachers!

Now, why aren't kids learning to read? Are children less intelligent today than fifty years ago? Surely we can't blame the children. We are expecting kids to read without giving them the tools necessary for reading. Some educators say that a student should not know a vowel before the third grade. No wonder kids can't read! They have not been given the tools: alphabet, vowels, consonants, blends, and diacritical marks. That is like expecting a surgeon to save lives through surgery without a thorough knowledge of anatomy. Such a surgeon would look for the appendix inside the skull!

In his book, **Why Johnny Can't Read,** Rudolph Flesch identified the source of our school troubles as being related to reading. He explains, "Now that I have gone through dozens and dozens of books on reading, I know how well it all fits together. The primers and readers are keyed to the textbooks on how to teach reading and the textbooks are all carefully written so that every teacher in the land is shielded from any information about how to teach children anything about letters and sounds."

It's very simple. Students can't read because teachers don't know how to teach reading! And teachers can't teach reading because the Teachers' Colleges decided it was not necessary. Donald Lambro said in, the **Conscience of a Young Conservative,** "Many of the old tried and true educational methods were discarded simply because they were old." Not very bright is it?

Edsel of Education

The same thing happened in the teaching of math. Lambro said,

"For example, since 1958 NSF (National Science Foundation) has spent some $17 million on the new-math concept to teach our youngsters abstract theories in mathematics instead of the essentials of how to add, subtract, divide, and multiply. The result, as surveys indicate, has been an entire class of young people who are incapable of performing such basic mathematical exercises as balancing a checkbook and computing a weekly salary." We have laws to protect animals from inhumane treatment yet permit the educational establishment to callously experiment with the minds of our children!

I have discovered that most students coming to our private, Christian school from public schools test at least one year behind their grade level in math. This is one of the results of experimentation with students in the new math, a multimillion dollar failure that was foisted upon school systems that are too quick to accept the newest fads. The new math, so readily accepted, was not adequately tested to measure its ultimate effect on students. In other words, our kids were used as guinea pigs without proper safeguards. The new math is the "Edsel" of education, but no one is held accountable for the blunder.

So, the problem is evident all along the line, from elementary into high school and right into college. The students are being robbed. They pay their taxes or tuition, and receive a counterfeit diploma.

Colleges are "giving the students whatever they want," according to a report issued by the Carnegie Foundation for the Advancement of Teaching. Students are permitted to take "Mickey Mouse" electives that will not challenge their minds but occupy their time and provide the necessary credit hours for graduation. (to do what - work at Disney World?) It seems the diploma is more important than knowledge.

The Report said that 1975 tests showed that 26 percent of entering freshmen at Ohio State University had not mastered high school math and 30 percent lacked acceptable college-level writing skills.

Teachers Fail Test

Maybe that is why many teachers cannot spell, write a coherent sentence, speak correct grammar or pass a general knowledge test. The Council for Basic Education reported that prospective school teachers in Pinellas County, Florida were tested for teaching jobs and two-thirds of them failed an eighth-grade level general knowledge test!

The Dallas School District decided to give a competency test to all beginning teachers and administrators to measure their mental ability. So, 535 new faculty members marched into the classrooms and took the test. Half of them failed to pass! What made it even more embarrassing was, the administrators did worse than the teachers!!

Well, no doubt, it was a poorly constructed test and impossible for anyone to pass. No, students at a private North Dallas high school took the test and did better than the public school teachers and administrators. Maybe they should hire the high school pupils and fire the incompetent state-trained teachers.

The Dallas school administration tried to cover up the scandal for three months and released the test results only after the Texas Attorney General ruled that the scores were public property.

I suggest those teachers demand a refund from the colleges where they were trained.

If the universities are bad then our whole society will be contaminated. Teachers are being graduated from college, certified but not qualified.

Mickey Mouse Courses

What are administrators and college trustees thinking when they approve such courses as Wayne State University's "Billiards and Pool"? The University of Iowa offers college credit for frisbee throwing and Ferris State College in Big Rapids, Michigan grants degrees in auto repair.

Max Rafferty reported in the **Indianapolis Star** on August 8, 1978, that Bowling Green University in Ohio is giving credit for riding roller coasters! Well, that may be consistent since most university students are being taken for a ride anyway. The University of Maryland has higher standards: they give credit for watching TV soap operas!

The University of California at San Diego offered a course in "Sand Castle Building" while Florida Atlantic University offered a more stimulating seminar on the "advantages of using **incorrect** English in the classroom."

The University of Arizona in Tucson offers Garbology 109; a class that meets at the city dump and sorts garbage! Professor William Rathje says, "We're talking about getting a total perspective on garbage." The class is referred to by the French term, "Le Project du Garbage." Of course, garbage by any other name still stinks.

One California State College offers such courses as Relevant Recreation in the Ghetto and The Selection and Preparation of Soul Food. Very intellectual!

Educational Quackery

Illinois State University offers credit in lawn-mowing. I am not sure whether it is push and pull type or self propelled tractor mowing. Michigan State University's Justin Morrill College is giving 15 hours of credit for a canoe trip down the Mississippi River! Or, how about a degree in Faith Healing from Oral Roberts University? Manhattanville College at Purchase, New York, gives credit for extracurricular activities and for a student's hobbies, while Evergreen State students received college credit for helping establish a city park.

A good example of educational quackery is recorded in **The Disaster Lobby** by Melvin Grayson and Thomas Shepard, Jr.: "In February of 1972, a state supported college opened for business above a Walgreen drug store in downtown St. Paul, Minnesota. It was called Metropolitan State College, and it had no lecture halls, no dormitories, no semesters, no-required courses and no grades. David Sweet, its 38-year-old first President nick-named it 'Wing-it-U.' " I'm afraid that most colleges could be called "Wing-it-U."

Quality Education

It would seem that clowns are running the universities and taxpayers are paying for the fun-time. It galls me to hear those who worship at the throne of public education talk of academic excellence and to hear them "put down" those private and Christian colleges who refuse accreditation because of principle. Please remember that all the aforementioned "schools of higher learning" are fully accreditated and approved by their respective states.

The state-approved academicians wax eloquent when they criticize the "unaccreditated" Christian colleges and proudly tell anyone within shouting distance that they alone are holding the line for quality education and intellectual honesty. But are they?

Geoffrey Wagner said in the July 23, 1972, issue of **National Review** that City College of New York did not require a high school diploma from some students! That's interesting. Most of us thought all state-approved colleges required a high school diploma.

Watered Down Standards

The **LC Reporter,** faculty organ for City University of New York (CUNY), reported concerning high school "graduates" who enrolled in that university: "To keep faith with our promise to these kids - that we'd give them a fair chance to make it in college instead of cynically proving to them that they can't - **we're watering down our standards.** (emphasis mine) Out of guilt for not teaching them properly, we're keeping them in college artificially." What an admission and from the official faculty organ! If those students are being kept in college "artificially," can we not honestly believe those students will receive an artificial degree? Approved, of course, but artificial just the same.

The **LC Reporter** did not report what a **New York Times** investigation revealed concerning CUNY and its faculty. Peter Witonski did report on it in his book, **What Went Wrong With American Education and How to Make It Right:** "The **New York Times** investigation revealed that educators and psychologists with Ph.D's from various unaccredited diploma mills presently hold high-ranking positions on the faculty and in the administration at CUNY and several other accredited New York universities." Well, well, well, you can be sure the college presidents don't talk about that when they beg the legislature for more money each year to finance their fun house.

It should be no surprise that public education is a "mess" when you realize that most teachers are a "mess," helped along by the above mentioned universities. Newly graduated teachers have been conned into believing they have been educated and are qualified to teach school. The results prove otherwise.

Schools Not Safe

Not only is a high percentage of public schools not doing an acceptable academic job, they are not even providing a safe place for kids to receive an inferior education. It is bad enough not to learn to read but incredible that the kids are raped, robbed and mugged.

Many school systems have hired armed guards to patrol the halls and rest rooms and even that is not working well. The Chicago **Tribune** reported in its January 7, 1978, issue on a study by the National Institute of Education: "The report noted that more than 5,000 secondary school teachers are attacked in an average month, almost 1,000 of whom require a doctor's attention." Notice that

5,000 per month are attacked! Any wonder concerned teachers are deserting the public schools?

The report also stated that almost 2.4 million students have something stolen from them each month. Well, the kids can't spell but they can surely steal! Of course, this goes back to the home and church but thievery is even encouraged at school. A textbook used in West Virginia asks, "Do you think it was right for Johnny to steal the penny from the mean grocer in this situation?" Now, with that wording, you know the student's response. The teacher is instructed to give no moral guidelines: "Don't try to impose your personal standards upon your students."

Now, it is all right for a teacher to impose her standards if she has no standards! She can't teach morality, but she can teach immorality. I wonder why?

Secular Humanism

The religion of the public schools is Secular Humanism. Secular Humanism is a religion as per two recent Supreme Court decisions. Humanism is based on the Humanist Manifesto I and II. It is interesting to note that John Dewey signed Manifesto I.

Humanism teaches that there is no heaven and no hell. In fact, such teaching is bad for young minds according to Humanists. Now, pornography in the text books is **not** harmful; hard core sex scenes on T.V. are **not** harmful; explicit sex education courses are **not** harmful, but the Bible teaching of a heaven to gain and a hell to shun is harmful. Very interesting.

A Humanist believes in abortion, mercy-killing, and suicide. So, you can see the Humanist is really concerned about people except "people" who happen to be still in the womb. Those can be slaughtered at taxpayer's expense. They also don't care too much for old people who tend to get in the way and "should be done away with." Notice that the Humanist is a coward since he wants to kill only babies and old people who can't defend themselves against the sanctimonious hypocrites. This is some of the "education" proffered by most schools to young kids.

The Secular Humanist believes the universe is selfexistent. He tells us that God did not create the world since God does not exist. One day, millions of years ago, the universe "just happened." That concept is almost as reasonable as looking at an intricate watch and affirming, "That watch 'just happened' one day."

Gospel of Evolution

The Humanist tells little children that man came from lower forms of life. They are dishonest when they talk of the "missing link" as if there are not thousands of "missing links." They never answer the question, "Where did life first appear and where did it come from?" They don't like to explain how the Second Law of Thermodynamics alone shuts the mouths of the evolutionists.

They don't like to talk of mountain tops covered with sea shells and remnants of a world flood. They don't want to admit that when Chuck Darwin fired a shot heard around the world, he fired a blank. They don't like to talk of Darwin's credentials as a scientist: he only possessed a divinity degree!

But they do conjure up in the minds of students, a modern ape swinging through the trees until he (it) became conscious of his mentality. He realized he was really only a very hairy, swinging Ph.D., so he swung to the ground saying, "Today, I am a man." Is it any wonder kids are acting like animals when they are taught that they came from animals?

Evolutionists don't want to talk of the fact that there has not been **one** fossil found of an intermediate link. The fossils prove that a dog is always a dog and a horse is always a horse. Any changes are **always** within the species.

The Humanists have had access to the public school system for almost 75 years, yet have not convinced a large segment of Americans that the universe and man "just happened." A scientific survey revealed that 86% of U.S. citizens preferred Creation and evolution to be taught on an equal basis in public schools instead of evolution alone. Only 8 ½ percent wanted evolution to have a monopoly in the public schools. Wonder what that 8 ½ percent are afraid of?

Evolution Pure Quackery

This guess of evolution has become, to some people, the gospel of evolution. College and high school teachers parrot what they heard in college to gullible students entrusted to their care: students who have not been taught to think for themselves. The teachers and students alike are standing on quicksand and will surely sink together as they quote the unholy trinity of Darwin, Huxley, and Spencer.

Evolution is pure quackery and purveyors of this foolishness should be branded as quacks. They are phony intellectuals and venders of ancient mythologies resurrected from Greece. Darwin and his ilk were not even original. They picked up old guess-work passed on to Plato and Aristotle. The Greeks had picked up evolution from the ancient Phoenicians.

Evolution is an old heathen corpse set up in a morgue. Charles Darwin and Herbert Spencer tried to modernize and beautify it. They dragged a 3,000 year old corpse around the world boasting that it was their discovery.

For Humanist textbooks to affirm that all scientists and most thinking men believe in evolution is a fraud and a lie. Hundreds of scientists do not believe in evolution. Dr. Albert Fleischman, professor of Zoology at the University of Erlangen in Germany, said, "The Darwinian theory has not a single fact to confirm it in the realm of nature. It is not the result of scientific research but purely the product of imagination."

God or Chuck Darwin

The Bible says, "The Lord God formed man from the dust of the ground and breathed into his nostrils the breath of life and man became a living soul." It takes less faith to accept this truth than the ridiculous speculation of organic evolution.

The Humanist tells students that God did not create the heaven and the earth, man and all things on the earth. Either He did or He did not. You may prefer the guess-work of Darwin, but you have lined up on the wrong side and the losing side. You see, Chuck Darwin was not present at the creation; God was, and I will take His Word as to what really occurred on that occasion.

Evolution is a "rope of sand," a chain of fog and a bridge of mist, yet it is taught in most public schools as a fact at the exclusion of special Creation that most taxpayers want taught. Is it any wonder intelligent people are fleeing the public schools?

Sex Education

Another reason thousands have fled the public schools is the teaching of sex education to kids in all grades starting with kindergarten. Usually, the course is a how-to course. A sane person would think that the schools would spend their time teaching reading and math instead of showing dirty movies to immature kids.

The most infamous pusher of pornography in American schools is a "kinky" group called, Sex Information and Education Council of the United States better known as SIECUS. The **St. Louis Globe-Democrat** identified SIECUS as "a kooky outfit."

The SIECUS Board is made up of respectable people who obviously don't know what is going on, including clergymen, psychologists, physicians, sociologists, and educators. Some of those associated with SIECUS have been identified as Communists or as having close ties to the Communist Party.

Those of us who don't mind being tagged as flag waving patriots have a knee-jerk reaction to those who are chummy with the Communists. We don't believe it is the better part of wisdom to smile benignly on those traitors who would march us off in chains to slave labor camps to the loud blaring of the Communist **Internationale.** Nor, is it intelligent, in the light of history, to pick up a shovel and dig a collective grave-like hole while Nikita Khrushchev's speech is being played over loud speakers. Not too bright is it?

Advice From A Sex Expert

The President of SIECUS is Dr. Mary S. Calderone. Dr. Calderone wrote in **Look** magazine, while giving advice to kids, saying you should "separate yourselves from your parents . . . Sex is not just something you do in marriage, in bed, in the dark, in one position." She told the students at Blair Academy in New Jersey, "I'm a religious person, but I don't believe the old 'Thou Shalt Nots' apply any more." Believe them or not, Mary, but the Author never repealed them, and you will face Him someday.

Dr. Albert Ellis, another leader in sex education, said concerning premarital sex, "You can catch a cold and you can lose a lot of sleep." I have news for you, Doc: kids are catching more than colds, and they are losing much more than sleep, like innocence, virginity, chances for a happy marriage, and in some cases, their lives by suicide.

Dr. Ellis said in the **Daily O'Collegian,** "Those who don't masturbate are the ones that are hung-up, not the ones who do." He went on to recommend premarital intercourse as "a good indoor diversion." Do you want such "professionals" writing material for your children?

Some kids in Manhatten are putting into practice what they learned in the classroom. Dr. Paul Cates and a New York pastor visited a Jr. High School in Manhatten, New York in the Fall of 1978 and observed a boy and girl having sex relations in the hall! Dr. Cates asked a teacher, "Aren't you going to do something about that?" The teacher replied, "No, there is nothing we can do about it. It happens often here. We can't interfere with a student's rights." Would the National Education Association call that good and proper sex education?

The principal stays all day in his office behind 3 locked doors, so he is very smart or very scared. Of course, his students are not permitted to pray and read the Bible in class since that might infringe on someone's rights. My question is: What about the rights of the decent kids who must live daily in that environment?

Sick or Chic

There are thousands of horror stories relating to sex education in the public schools throughout America. Usually, the teacher determines just how obnoxious the class becomes. In Evanston, Illinois, a ten-year-old girl eating dinner with her family calmly said, "Well, we had a good time discussing the penis in school today." I suppose some parents think that is "chic" for a 10 year old, but I don't think it is "chic"; I think it is sick. A ten-year-old girl should be discussing dolls, mixed fractions, and T.V. cartoons, but not the penis.

Gloria Lentz said in **Raping Our Children**, "A high school teacher in Van Nuys, California asks his students about their personal participation in such activities as masturbation, fondling breasts or genitals, sexual intercourse, homosexual activities, and sexual activity with animals. The American Education Lobby claims that these are not isolated cases but are typical of what is taking place with increasing frequency in classrooms all across America."

Is the above going on in your school system? You may be surprised. Have you tried to find out? After all, the schools belong to you, not the administrators, the teachers, the politicians, or the Teachers' Union. You are paying the bills and have a right to know what is being taught to your children.

Sex Taught With Morality

Sex education should be taught in the home by parents who love and understand their children. Morality and sex must be taught together with the parents' moral values being reflected and not the amoral and immoral philosophy of some humanistic, money grubbing, sex pushing organizations.

Most parents agree with Dr. William McGrath who said, "Details of mating and reproduction are not the facts of life for a child and should not be. One does not turn the sixth grader loose in a machine shop or in a college chemistry laboratory."

Dr. McGrath continued, "Premature interest in sex is unnatural and will arrest or distort the development of the personality . . . Anyone who would deliberately arouse the child's curiosity or stimulate his unready mind to troubled sexual preoccupations ought to have a millstone tied around his neck and be cast into the sea."

McGrath was only repeating what Christ said about those who harm children. Those who warp the young minds of kids are the ultimate child abusers, and I would be honored to affix the millstones, starting with the SIECUS leaders and then to the school superintendents and teachers who are sex-pushers. But, I'm afraid I would run out of millstones.

Sex Pushers and The Results

These "professionals" presented sex education to us parents as being noble, cultural, and the answer to teen-age pregnancies, venereal disease, and abortion. Of course, all these problems have skyrocketed since the inception of sex education. Meanwhile, the sex pushers laugh all the way to the bank while parents try to pick up the pieces of broken and ruined lives of their children.

Since sex education is here, children don't have to hear vulgar, four-letter words from older boys in back alleys. They can now hear the same four-letter words in the classrooms from their teachers. They receive detailed instructions on how to perform. There have been incidents of kids as young as 4 attacking younger sisters. We were told that sex education would not stimulate but educate. But experiences have proved that kids go even further and try to procreate.

Sex education was to be uplifting, yet it has become degrading. Isn't it degrading to hear 5 year-old kids using gutter terms describing the penis and intercourse? Isn't it degrading to have kindergarten and first grade kids climbing upon each other to demonstrate how mom and dad "make a baby"? Isn't it degrading to see little kids on a field trip to a farm inspecting the reproductive organs of the animals rather than appreciating the animals themself?

Is it strange then, that children act like animals when they are taught a no-holds-barred sex course by people who are not permitted to tie morality to the lessons being taught? In fact, the teachers often are single teachers only a couple years out of college. Some of them have taken a six or eight week course and have become sex experts!

Teacher Raped By Students

Other teachers have had shattering experiences with sex education students. Clinton Thamer wrote an article headed: "Students Rape Teacher to Pass Sex Education Exams." The story was a grisly tale of a young teacher who was raped by twenty grade school boys in her own classroom! (Remember, the sex-pushers told us that sex information, even vivid films and slides, will not stimulate students!) One of the boys involved in the attack said, "We didn't think we were doing anything wrong . . . didn't she spend the whole year telling us how to do it, when to do it, and how much fun it would be?"

The boy, although trying to justify his reprehensible actions, did ask a good question. Indeed, what did any sane person expect but exactly what happened? It is one thing to teach a boy to drive a car but just as important are the rules of the road. How fast may he drive? What does he do at a four-way stop? What about passing cars? How close does he follow the other cars? We have been teaching kids the mechanics of sex without any "rules of the road" to give them guidelines. We would be fools to expect anything but a moral pile-up.

Gloria Lentz in her book, **Raping Our Children,** quoted Dr. William A. Marra, professor of Philosophy at Fordham University for fourteen years, as saying concerning sex education: "I say many of the slides remind me of nothing more than latrine art - that I would be horrified to have any of my children look at a woman with her legs spread apart and erections and ejaculations. I would say the people advancing this are sick."

Sex Not Dirty

"Well, I insist, that we parents . . . in no way believe sex is dirty, but we believe it is private and intimate . . . It is quite tactful for you to go to a party and talk about your tonsils. It is not tactful - it is not acceptable - for you to go to a party and talk about how your wife makes love to you, not because you think it is dirty, my friends, but because you think it is intimate."

That perfectly expresses my attitude on sex education as well as millions of others who take time to inquire what sex education is all about. When some parents, who were at first supporters of sex education, discovered what was being taught to their children, they became leaders in the movement to drive sex education out of the public schools. But, some educators are determined to teach your children sex even in kindergarten and even if it is at variance with your own moral standards. Is it any wonder concerned parents are fleeing the public schools?

Double Standard

Some principals have permitted children to be excused from sex education classes if their parents objected - loudly. Some kids stood outside the classroom while others sat in the office and still others went to a study hall. But, why should a child's education be "put on hold" while kids of permissive or uninformed parents are watching a dirty movie? We are told the exclusion from class is an acceptable second choice. I don't think so. Why not continue with proper education and show sex slides and movies at night to those students who are interested? How many teachers would **volunteer** to teach under those circumstances?

So, our kids should stand outside the class during sex education and it won't hurt them, so say the liberals. But, what about kids who object to Bible reading and patriotic ceremonies? Should they be excused and made to stand in the halls? Oh! No! That will bruise their ego; so stop the Bible reading and patriotic ceremonies.

This double standard is perfectly illustrated by an incident that took place in Indiana recently. Max W. Lynch taught Math at the Indiana State University Laboratory School in Terre Haute. Max added some Bible reading to his math lessons. He was also fired after refusing to stop the Bible reading. He discovered that academic freedom didn't go **that** far.

Bible Outlawed

The First District Appeals Court ruled unanimously to support a lower court's ruling that he be fired. Max pleaded that any objecting student could leave the room until the reading was finished as some students do when sex is being taught. But the court said that the student's freedom to leave the class was severely limited by "peer pressure, fear of the teacher and the alternative of standing outside the classroom in the hall."

The Court went on to say that Lynch's alternative for the students would have a "chilling effect at best and, more likely, a coercive impact on the students' free exercise of their religious rights."

Let me see if I understand: It is not harmful for an objecting student to stand in the hall during a sex education class, but it is harmful and has a "chilling effect" if a student stands outside the room during Bible reading. I still don't think I understand. Maybe some liberal out there can explain it to me, but I won't count on it.

System Falling Apart

Even a fool is aware that the public schools are in trouble; some would say even the last gasps are audible over the ravings of the NEA that American students have never had it so good. It is the administrators and teachers who have never had it so good. The system is falling apart as the seams split open, but fools keep trying to patch things up with more money.

Most informed people would say that there is no hope. The union bosses have a death grip on the throat of the public schools. When the unions aren't choking the life from the schools, the federal judges do their thing and we have affirmative action, busing, and other prescriptions written by fools or madmen.

New teachers have been inadequately taught and too many are motivated by money. This is evident as teachers leave their classrooms unsupervised as they walk a picket line demanding more money, less work, and wanting to tell their employer, the schools boards, how to run the schools!

An Answer

Do I have any suggestions for change? You bet. Pay teachers according to merit, not according to years in the classroom; but pay them well. Eliminate tenure since incompetent teachers are kept on the payroll - forever. Good teachers are not afraid of losing their jobs, and they want to see the incompetent teachers booted out of the schools.

Scratch collective bargaining laws whereby union bosses almost run the schools. Fire all teachers who strike and refuse to rehire them. Supervise the teaching and demand and get quality education in every classroom.

As administrators enter retirement, die or move away, don't replace them. Most school systems have too many chiefs running around.

The **Review of the News** for June 21, 1978 reported: "In Chicago, 46 percent of the school system's staff are 'support staff' who have nothing to do with teaching." The article reported that Detroit had 50 percent, while New Orleans and Indianapolis had 49% of supervisors on their staffs.

I wonder how many of those administrators ever taught in a classroom. Many are good at "chewing out" young teachers who need guidance; shuffling papers; and flushing the "johns"; but are bumbling incompetents in front of a fifth grade class. No administrator should ever be hired who has not spent at least two years in a classroom.

Gut the educational departments in the colleges since most of the courses are a waste of time. Get back to teaching teachers how to teach and what to teach. Challenge prospective teachers to dedicate their lives to helping kids make a life as well as a living. Convey to teachers that what they are is much more important than what they say.

Bible and Discipline

Return Bible morality to the schools; not a particular denomination but simple Bible teaching and prayer. Let each school system reflect the general religious philosophy of the area. (i.e. Catholics, Baptist, Amish, etc.). Patriotism, unabashed, flag waving patriotism should be promoted every day in every class. Fire all Communists, fellow travelers, Black Nationalists, and other anti-Americans! Fire any woman who gets pregnant before she sees the preacher. Do the same for all sodomites and lesbians.

Demand discipline in every class. Expel those students who refuse to obey the rules. Restore a dress code to the schools for teachers and students. Hold parents accountable for all vandalism perpetrated by their children.

For students who want to learn and will co-operate with the teachers and administrators, I suggest they be taught on their own achievement level, not on what grade they have advanced to by a foolish system of social promotion. Social promotion has been a smoke screen to hide a failing system, but the smoke has cleared away and we now realize the folly.

Success in Class

Every student should be tested and diagnosed and an educational prescription be written for each child. If he is in the seventh grade but doing fifth grade work, leave him in the seventh grade, but put him to work on a fifth grade level. He will discover that he can do the work! Success is his for the first time in years.

Of course, this will require a personalized curriculum, re-training of teachers and much more work, but it is the only answer for students who have huge gaps in their learning. A student should not be permitted to proceed in his material until he has mastered it. He should be required to set goals each day and be checked daily to make sure he reaches the goals set for that day.

A typical seventh grade student will be working at various levels: He may be working on seventh grade social studies, sixth grade English, and fifth grade math and science. It is foolish and tragic to assume that a seventh grade student is capable of seventh grade work in all subjects. He **should** be working at seventh grade level, but it is not realistic under prevailing circumstances. It is also tragic to assume that all seventh grade students (or sixth grade, etc.) are on the same level. This is done only as an administrative convenience with the kids paying the price.

Cut the Frills

Eliminate the "frill" courses that are not really essential but are very costly. Kids often spend their day at school drawing, sawing, pounding, driving, playing, cooking, running errands and swimming. They are there to receive a basic education, and they are not getting it. We built a great nation, producing a generation of leaders, in schools without driver's education, swimming pools, tennis courts, shops and cooking classes.

The taxpayers are fed up with gargantuan costs of education or more appropriately: mis-education. They wouldn't mind paying exorbitant taxes if kids were reading, if the schools were safe, and if the expensive buildings were not shells a' la post war Germany. But, we say that there must be a limit as to what we can afford. The dollar only goes so far, and we who pay the freight say that too many dollars have been poured down a rathole on monstrous, expensive buildings, excessive administrative personnel, and numerous frill courses. Let's really get back to basics and provide relief (spelled C-U-T F-A-T) for the overburdened taxpayers and good, sound education for our children.

Compulsory Attendance Bad

Now, I want to take a swing at the most sacred cow of all - compulsory attendance laws. In a word, repeal them. At least, permit a student to drop out of school at age 14. I believe a student has a civil right to be a bum if he wants to be a bum. If he won't behave and do his work, boot him out of school. That way, those kids who want an education can get one. Teachers will also live longer.

Even liberal Paul Goodman said in his **Compulsory Mis-education,** "The compulsory system has become a universal trap, and it is no good." Schools have become a trap to hundreds of thousands of kids; a trap that is sprung at age 16. Free the trouble-making kids; students who want to learn; and the teachers by repealing compulsory attendance laws.

Max Rafferty said it right: "A school is neither a health resort, a recreation center, nor a psychiatric clinic. It's a place where the massed wisdom of the ages is passed from one generation to the next, and where youngsters are taught to think in a logical and systematic fashion. A school where subject disciplines are unimportant is a school where education itself has become irrelevant."

If we put some of these principles suggested in this chapter into practice, we will again produce a generation of leaders; leaders with character. After all, we only have one chance at educating our children. We had better do it right the first time or we will lose our kids and our nation. If we do it right, we will raise a generation of kids that will be happy and not hippy. Our nation can not afford to fail another generation. But the hour is late. We must act now.

Patrick Henry had put his name on the line. He stepped up and stood toe to toe with tyranny. He looked King George in the eyes and didn't blink. He made his position clear to all those in that august Virginia Assembly as they debated the necessity for separation from England and the implications of freedom.

Thousands have followed that rallying cry of Henry's but please remember an unnamed Baptist pastor in Culpepper, Virginia, as he staggered home weak from loss of blood to his family. His act of obedience to God triggered the oration of Patrick Henry.

Liberty is From God

Thomas Jefferson said, "The God who gave us life, gave us liberty." Liberty is one of the sweetest words in any language. Liberty means each person is free to be different from everyone else. A man is free to be himself. If I am free simply to be like others, or to do as others, then obviously I am not free.

The Psalmist said in Psalms 119:45, *"And I will walk at liberty."* We have been walking free for over 200 years because we obeyed God's precepts. Verse 47 says, *"And I will delight myself in thy commandments, which I have loved."* Do we still love His commandments?

America has been great because she has been good. She has been free because she has been faithful. But, America is becoming less faithful and, consequently, less free. We are not as good as we have been and we are not as great.

National Weaknesses

I must not dwell on our weaknesses to prove the point. Our nation is staggering under a national debt that is so astronomical, only a handful of economists can comprehend the enormity of the problem. This problem is compounded because many of the economists and politicians don't even recognize it as a major problem.

Our people are so insecure they are reaching out for security in a bottle, and we have a national scandal with millions of alcoholics, including a growing number of pre-teens. Even worse, babies are being born with a dependence on booze because Mom was a boozer!

Venereal disease is epidemic in all ages, especially teenagers as they emulate the promiscuity of their parents and follow the crowds as they chant, "Do your own thing; whatever feels good is right."

Along with this promiscuity go the unwanted pregnancies,

Patrick Henry had put his name on the line. He stepped up and stood toe to toe with tyranny. He looked King George in the eyes and didn't blink. He made his position clear to all those in that august Virginia Assembly as they debated the necessity for separation from England and the implications of freedom.

Thousands have followed that rallying cry of Henry's but please remember an unnamed Baptist pastor in Culpepper, Virginia, as he staggered home weak from loss of blood to his family. His act of obedience to God triggered the oration of Patrick Henry.

Liberty is From God

Thomas Jefferson said, "The God who gave us life, gave us liberty." Liberty is one of the sweetest words in any language. Liberty means each person is free to be different from everyone else. A man is free to be himself. If I am free simply to be like others, or to do as others, then obviously I am not free.

The Psalmist said in Psalms 119:45, *"And I will walk at liberty."* We have been walking free for over 200 years because we obeyed God's precepts. Verse 47 says, *"And I will delight myself in thy commandments, which I have loved."* Do we still love His commandments?

America has been great because she has been good. She has been free because she has been faithful. But, America is becoming less faithful and, consequently, less free. We are not as good as we have been and we are not as great.

National Weaknesses

I must not dwell on our weaknesses to prove the point. Our nation is staggering under a national debt that is so astronomical, only a handful of economists can comprehend the enormity of the problem. This problem is compounded because many of the economists and politicians don't even recognize it as a major problem.

Our people are so insecure they are reaching out for security in a bottle, and we have a national scandal with millions of alcoholics, including a growing number of pre-teens. Even worse, babies are being born with a dependence on booze because Mom was a boozer!

Venereal disease is epidemic in all ages, especially teenagers as they emulate the promiscuity of their parents and follow the crowds as they chant, "Do your own thing; whatever feels good is right."

Along with this promiscuity go the unwanted pregnancies,

VIII

MUST CHRISTIANS ALWAYS OBEY THE LAW?

A Christian lawyer was riding his horse through his home state of Virginia. He was going home. The young lawyer often had printed gospel tracts and distributed them to his friends and associates. He often defended preachers in the courtrooms of Virginia without asking or expecting remuneration.

As he rode into Culpeper he saw something that made his blood run cold. A crowd had gathered in the square and was watching a Baptist preacher being tied to a flogging pole. The pastor was a serious law breaker, for Virginia had a law forbidding anyone to preach without a license, and he was not licensed! That preacher knew he needed only the call of God and not the approval of the state, so he refused to be licensed.

During those early years before the War of 1776, hundreds of men paid a dear price to proclaim the faith "once for all delivered to the saints." The young attorney watched as that pastor was beaten until his back was raw. As the blood flowed, something clicked in the mind of that Christian lawyer. As he rode home, the event in Culpeper kept turning in his mind.

Liberty or Death

When the attorney arrived home, he sat at his desk and penned a few words that would become a rallying cry for patriots and on March 23, 1778, at St. John's Episcopal Church in Williamsburg, Virginia, he spat out those words for the world to hear: "Is life so dear, or peace so sweet as to be purchased at the price of chains and slavery? Forbid it Almighty God! I know not what course others may take, but as for me give me liberty or give me death." There, Patrick Henry said in public what many were saying in private.

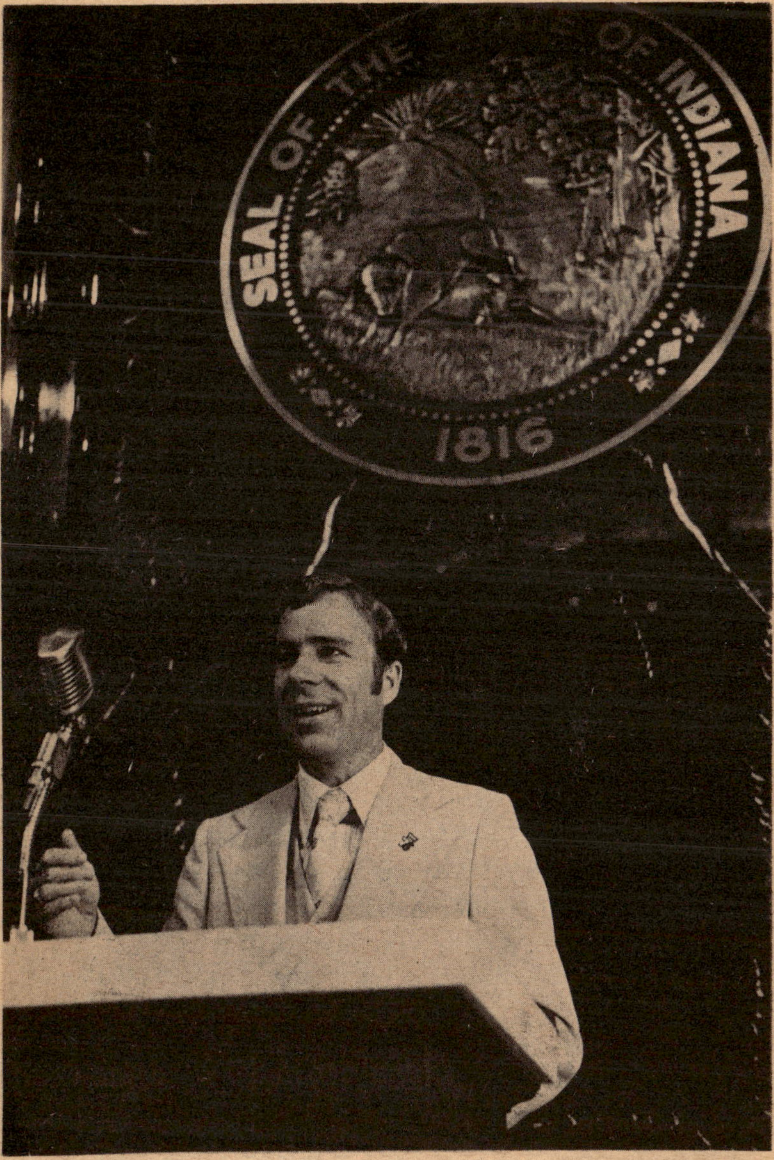
SEAL OF THE STATE OF INDIANA
1816

good, sound education for our children.

Compulsory Attendance Bad

Now, I want to take a swing at the most sacred cow of all - compulsory attendance laws. In a word, repeal them. At least, permit a student to drop out of school at age 14. I believe a student has a civil right to be a bum if he wants to be a bum. If he won't behave and do his work, boot him out of school. That way, those kids who want an education can get one. Teachers will also live longer.

Even liberal Paul Goodman said in his **Compulsory Mis-education,** "The compulsory system has become a universal trap, and it is no good." Schools have become a trap to hundreds of thousands of kids; a trap that is sprung at age 16. Free the trouble-making kids; students who want to learn; and the teachers by repealing compulsory attendance laws.

Max Rafferty said it right: "A school is neither a health resort, a recreation center, nor a psychiatric clinic. It's a place where the massed wisdom of the ages is passed from one generation to the next, and where youngsters are taught to think in a logical and systematic fashion. A school where subject disciplines are unimportant is a school where education itself has become irrelevant."

If we put some of these principles suggested in this chapter into practice, we will again produce a generation of leaders; leaders with character. After all, we only have one chance at educating our children. We had better do it right the first time or we will lose our kids and our nation. If we do it right, we will raise a generation of kids that will be happy and not hippy. Our nation can not afford to fail another generation. But the hour is late. We must act now.

illegitimate births, "shot gun" weddings, life times of misery, and the slaughter of hundreds of thousands of babies in abortion mills.

Couples procure a marriage license and enter into the holy state of matrimony with less thought than they give to the brand of mouthwash they will purchase. Later, they will decide marriage was a bad trip and make their way to the divorce courts, without bad breath of course.

Need I dwell on the incredible increases in juvenile delinquency, suicides, the crime rate, and race hatred? What about the pitiful education received by kids today in a nation that spends each year more and more on education to get less and less? Must I point to the multiplicity of churches and religions simultaneously present with the abject loss of power in our personal lives to overcome the evil one?

Can You Remember

Can you remember back when our nation was great? Can you remember:
When our schools were peaceful?
When our cities were safe?
When girls never hitched rides with strangers?
When criminals were in jail, not hospitals or country clubs?
When degenerates were still in the closets?
When babies were born out of wedlock, but there was shame and regret?
When a man went to a hospital for a couple weeks if he ridiculed the flag? - When he was buried if he spat on it?
When Americans traveled overseas and were respected and admired?
When we kept our national commitments to our friends?
When our enemies had a healthy fear of the United States of America?
When you could watch T.V. and never hear God's name taken in vain and not see a bedroom scene all week?
When you could afford to eat steak once a week?
When you could get a job done right for a reasonable price?
When a man had hair on his chest and bone in his back?
When teachers, policemen, and firefighters never carried picket signs?
When welfare was for the elderly, the sick, and the blind, not the young, the healthy and the lazy?

When a young man asked permission to marry a man's daughter?
When men defended their country and felt it was their sacred duty?
When you could mail a letter for 3 cents, and it didn't take a week to be delivered?
When churches of most denominations gave a public invitation for folk to accept Christ as Lord and Saviour?

Less Faithful - Less Free

Yes, we have become less faithful, and we are now less free. Woodrow Wilson said, "Liberty has never come from government . . . the history of liberty is the history of the limitations of governmental power, not the increase of it." The more dependence upon government the less freedom we will enjoy. The state may appear to be benevolent as it reaches out a velvet hand to help, but I must remind you that a mailed fist is hidden inside that velvet glove.

The central question in this state and nation is: "Shall we have controlled citizens or controlled government?" I suggest, no, I affirm, that government growth is out of control and with that growth goes our liberty.

In Pennsylvania a farmer must get a permit to plow his own fields! In Dade County, Florida, a man must get a permit if he paints his house using over $15.00 worth of paint! A teacher in Virginia, Laben Johnson, has suggested, as have others, that parents should be licensed to have children! Our forefathers fought the American Revolution for less odious governmental audacity.

Have we become a nation of sheep being led and controlled by governmental sheep dogs who do more barking than biting? Weak appeasers will say, "But, we need to go along in order to get along. Don't rock the boat; after all, the state has a heavy hand. There is something to be said for safety." So they tell us.

Ben Franklin had something to say about liberty and safety. He said, "They that can give up essential liberty to obtain a little temporary safety deserve neither liberty or safety."

If I must choose between liberty and safety, I will choose liberty every time.

Surrender our Freedom

Some liberal politicians think liberty is passé as a practical concept. They tell us we must surrender our freedom for the good of society, not all at once, just a little at a time. Because the loss is gradual, we don't see the peril.

Americans are like a bull frog. The frog reacts to a sudden movement, reading it as a threat. Americans do the same. We react to wars, earthquakes, famines, and storms because they are a threat to our existence.

But, like the frog, we don't react to threats that come gradually. Put the frog in a pan of water on the kitchen stove and turn up the heat. It won't jump out. Turn the heat higher until the vapor curls up around the frog's nostrils. The stupid frog will sit there and boil in the pan. Not very smart is it?

Americans are reacting the same way the frog reacts. We aren't reacting to the loss of freedom because, like the frog in the boiling water, the loss is not sudden but slow. So, we don't feel threatened. If war were declared on us tomorrow, we would react, maybe. But we can't see the threat to us from government intrusion into our lives and professions, more regulations, more taxes and bigger government. So we cook in our own juice. Maybe we deserve it.

Threats to Freedom

There are many threats to our freedom today and one is coming directly from the Carter White House. The President signed Executive Order 12053 dated April 14, 1978, to establish a Commission on the International Year of the Child. This will be to children what the International Women's Year was to women!

According to **Freedom Line,** July-August 1978 edition, this will be an effort to coincide with the United Nation's resolution of December 21, 1976, that declared 1979 as the International Year of the Child.

Congressman Robert K. Dornan of California wrote me saying, ". . . let me just give you . . . examples of what might happen under this U.N.-sponsored program:

"Children may gain the legal right to sue their parents for being forced to attend church (and the government would pay the lawyers!)." How does that grab you?

"Children who perform household chores may become eligible for minimum wage." Minimum wage for cutting the grass, taking out the garbage and washing the dishes!

"Public schools would conduct 'behavior modification' programs, possibly under U.N. supervision, to make American children better world citizens."

I don't want the federal government or the U.N. trying to modify the mind of my child. I prefer the behavior modification found in Phillippians 2:5, *"Let this mind be in you which was also in Christ Jesus."*

Government is Not God

The Psalmist said, "I will walk at liberty." I will walk a free man and not crawl on my knees to any government entity. I do not see government as my enemy, but I also don't see it as my God.

The storm clouds have been gathering over many states in recent years reminiscent of the 1700's, and it appears that there will be years of rough weather for churches, Christian schools and related ministries. The central issue is control. Will God's people control their ministries or will the state and federal government?

The states are trying to license churches and schools as they would plumbers, lawyers, physicians and auto mechanics. Just a little problem here. They have no authority to regulate churches. The authorities don't like to hear that, but there can be no compromise for temporary safety. It must be clear to all. The state has assumed power it does not have relating to licensure of churches and Christian schools. The Constitution says, "Congress shall make no law." What was that? "No law."

Let's clear the air with some truths.

A license does not guarantee protection for the children in a school, camp or children's home.

Children are a heritage of the Lord. They do not belong to the state.

A state cannot decide what is a legitimate ministry of the church and what is not.

States can't even handle the public schools, let alone Christian schools.

Churches and pastors are not being stubborn and hard to get along with. It is a scriptural conviction that if one must get a license, then someone is over him besides God. In fact, the states would tell you they are over God.

God Speaks on Church and State

Acts 5 records an interesting experience of Church-State conflict. Christ had recently been crucified, raised from the dead, and had ascended into heaven. The disciples had been filled with the Holy

Spirit and were performing miracles and preaching in great power until the whole city was buzzing with the talk of what was happening.

People were coming from the country to Jerusalem bringing the sick to be healed and "they were healed every one." (I don't know any faith healer in America who claims to heal everyone). When the local parsons saw the crowds coming to hear the "unlicensed" preachers, "they were filled with indignation." It didn't matter that thousands of sick folk were healed and thousands were saved; they wanted the preachers in jail. Sound familiar?

The apostles were put in jail, but God broke them out and told them to "Go, stand and speak . . . all the words of this life." They did, but the local council grabbed them again and asked, "Did not we straitly command you that ye should not teach in this name?" (Jesus)

Peter said, "We ought to obey God rather than men." That is the heart of the matter. Whenever there is a conflict, "we must obey God rather than men." Always? Always!

Christians are law-abiding people. That is part of our nature and our teaching. Jesus said, in Matthew 22:21, *"Render therefore unto Caesar the things which are Caesar's: and unto God the things that are God's."* That means, we pay our taxes, vote, obey the law and generally do what good citizens do. It does not mean the state owns us, nor does it mean the state is our god. It is a sin not to give Caesar what is due him, but it is also a sin to give Caesar what belongs to God. The big problem in many states is that caesar is trying to tell Christians what belongs to God and what belongs to Caesar. We can never permit that.

God's Authority

The state has almost become an object of worship and demands complete and unquestioned obedience from its citizens. We are to obey the law and respect and obey those in authority over us for all authority is from God. I believe when you meet a policeman, you meet God's authority.

In the home, the man is the authority representing God, and he is to be respected and obeyed. Now, it doesn't mean he is always right. It does not mean he is to beat his wife three or four times a week. I have found that once a week will accomplish as much and is less tiring. (To the libbers out there, I must add that I am kidding.

Sensible people are aware of that, but libbers have not only lost their sense but their sense of humor as well.)

But, the husband, the policeman, the judge, the pastor are all delegated authorities and do not deserve and require unqualified obedience. Only God receives unqualified obedience. Let me give you some examples: Pharaoh gave an order that all male babies born to the Israelites in Egypt would be slain. He so informed the Hebrew midwives. The king had spoken but so had God. God said that the murder of innocent children was wrong. So the ladies refused because it says in Exodus 1:17, *"the midwives feared God."* Folk don't fear God much anymore do they?

We Won't Bow

During the days of the Captivity some Jews had been taken from Jerusalem to Babylon along with the spoils of battle and some of them became politicians under King Nebuchadnezzar. The king ordered all his federal employees to bow to his statue. Three young Hebrews refused to do so, because God had told them in Exodus 20:5 *"Thou shalt not bow down thyself"* (to images). Here, in Daniel 3, was a conflict between government and God, and God won.

The three men were thrown bound into a furnace of fire, but God brought them out without the smell of smoke on their clothes and not a hair was singed! The only thing they lost in the fire was the ropes that bound them. No doubt there were people standing with them on the Plain of Dura who told them they had to obey the king, but the young Jews said, "We have to obey God." They owed the king obedience only as long as his commands did not conflict with God's. Most people are bowing before the image of the state.

In chapter six of Daniel, a law was passed that forbade anyone to pray for a thirty day period to any god or make a request to any man except the king. Anyone who broke that law went to a den of lions: a one way trip. Daniel was another Jew who had become a leading politician in Babylon, and this law had been passed to "get him." That's not the only time unreasonable laws have been passed to "get" God's people.

Daniel Disobeyed

Daniel, who prayed three times a day, was told about the new law and was asked his reaction and his plans. Daniel said, with a wry grin, "Fellows, I'll have to pray about that new law." And he did:

with his windows open, facing Jerusalem, he defied the law and prayed. Daniel the prophet and politician became the prisoner, but not for long, because God shut the mouths of the lions.

Daniel slept well that night in the lion's den probably using Leo as a pillow. In fact, the king could not sleep and went to the den of lions early in the morning to find Daniel, not dead, but sleeping. When Christians go to jail for their convictions, I believe they will rest better on a jail cot than the Governor will in his mansion. You see, the king was wrong. He did not deserve unquestioned obedience. Daniel respectfully defied the king, stood his ground and won his case. He would have been just as noble had he been devoured by the lions.

Daniel decided that it was better and safer to be in the company of the lions in obedience to God than disobey God and be in the palace. Too many Christians want to be "in the palace where the action is" licking the boots of the powers that be. We are not commanded to lick their boots; just obey government when it does not conflict with the commands of God.

Modern Quislings

Many religious leaders try to hide their cowardice by insisting on "obeying the law in every respect." That way, they don't have to take a firm position that may cost them their freedom, their money, and their reputation. They forget that Christ, "made Himself of no reputation" and went to jail as a criminal. Paul, Peter and other great preachers went to jail for their convictions. Most preachers don't have any trouble because they don't have any convictions.

Some pastors even take a stand against their colleagues who do stand for principle. They run ads in the newspapers identifying with the state and self righteously condemn those who stand for Biblical separation and the separation of church and state. These are modern day quislings who will do anything for a little temporary safety, slavishly accepting every governmental edict as if it came from Mt. Sinai instead of Capitol Hill.

Those men need to be reminded of the truth in the following verse:

No man escapes when freedom fails,
The best men rot in filthy jails,
And those who cried, "Appease! Appease!"
Are hanged by those they tried to please.

Principle of Authority

We are to obey every law of man as long as it is not in direct disobedience to God. Romans 13:1 says, *"Let every soul be subject unto the higher powers. For there is no power but of God: the powers that be are ordained of God."* Some people would tell us that this verse does not allow for any disobedience, but they overlook the principle of authority that says, "Only God receives unqualified obedience."

Christians must not use this principle to justify illegal activity such as civil rights marches, tying up traffic and inflicting their convictions on others who are not interested. We are to obey the laws we don't agree with as long as the laws are not unscriptural.

I need to remind you that the Apostle Paul, who wrote Romans, was himself a prisoner in Rome for his faithfulness to Christ. So, the one who was the human author of Rom. 13:1 was not "subject to the higher powers" when they conflicted with the really Higher Power. Paul's faithfulness cost him his life. A man's convictions can get him in some uncomfortable circumstances sometimes.

So, it is obvious that Christians should not always obey the law.

Preacher Goes to Jail

John Bunyon lived in Bedford, England in the mid 1600's and became a Christian and member of a separatist church. Soon, he felt called to preach, and he started doing just that. Just a little problem here; he was not licensed. The authorities told him to apply for a license, but John could not find scriptural authority for a license from the government so he refused.

John continued to preach even after he had been warned that prison would result in refusing the proffered license. Finally, he was arrested and incarcerated in the damp, cold, Bedford jail.

The authorities placed a preaching license beside his cell door. John could reach through the bars at any time and take the license and freedom. The decision was his: he could have liberty with a license or he could have his convictions with confinement. He chose the latter.

He had a daughter who came outside the prison and pleaded with him: "Come home; Momma needs you. We miss you, Daddy." John's convictions would not change for prison, for family, for country or death. Convictions are unchanging and unchangeable. One daughter died while he was in jail.

They brought him a bottle of clabbered milk twice a week that would normally go to the hogs. Each day, John peeled the paper cap off the bottle, spread it out and used it as writing paper. He took soot from the stone walls and, mixing it with water, made ink. During his 13 years in prison, he wrote one of the world's greatest books, **Pilgrim's Progress.**

Rats Ate License

From time to time, John looked at the license on the floor by his cell. That license meant home, family, home cooking, respectability, comfort, and freedom. It also meant compromise and cowardice. John was in jail for a principle, not as a "lark." It was not a weekend in jail as some liberals have had who get arrested for protesting every attempt America makes to build bombs, missiles, or nuclear power plants. Bunyon spent almost 13 years in Bedford jail.

The license was eaten by rats four times. The authorities visited Mrs. Bunyon and asked her to use her influence to get John to "take the license." She replied, as she held up her apron, "I would rather have John's head in my apron than have him be disloyal to his convictions and disobedient to Christ." John's wife was not the typical American housewife who sits around all day watching T.V. make-believes, playing bridge, and feeding her face with fudge.

Finally, John was released from jail. The license, half eaten by rats, was still on the floor beside his cell door. And, when Bunyon walked out of prison into the streets of Bedford a free man, he had made it possible for any farm boy in England to preach the gospel of Christ on any street corner - without a license.

No, a Christian should not always obey the law.

Brownstown Rally for Religious Freedom
over 2,000 people

IX

SHOULD CIVILIZED NATIONS EXECUTE KILLERS?

Tolstoy said, "The seeds of every vice are in each of us." Was that his way of saying that all men are born with a sinful nature necessitating a new nature in Jesus Christ?

Ernest Van Den Haag wrote in the March 27, 1977, **Indianapolis Star,** "The threats of the law are needed to prevent them (seeds of vice) from flowering, to control crime, to enforce the rules indispensable to moral and to social life."

Van was right. We need the threats of the law, but those threats must be carried out swiftly and firmly on all who defy the law. But the crime rate keeps climbing because law breakers are not being punished. Less than one percent of all crimes committed in the U.S. eventually leads to a prison sentence.

A potential felon must know that the law has teeth in it and will "bite his head off" if he tries to make crime pay. I must keep my promises to my children or they will never believe me. I must also carry out my threats. If I threaten to spank them if they "do that one more time," I must carry out my threat or my kids will know they can get away with murder. Criminals know they can get away with murder. Criminals must be convinced that crime does not pay. Our courts must see that criminals pay with their lives for capital crimes.

Fear of Hanging

Judge J. F. Stephen wrote, "Some men probably abstain from murder because they fear . . . that they would be hanged. Hundreds of thousands abstain from it because they regard it with horror. One reason they regard it with horror is that murderers are hanged."

However, we are not hanging killers anymore, and we are experiencing 20,000 murders each year. M. Stanton Evans' regular column in the **Indianapolis News** targeted in on the costs in murders each year because we don't have capital punishment.

Evans said, "For roughly a decade until the Gary Gilmore case, there had been no capital punishment in the United States, and the resulting toll of carnage speaks eloquently for itself. From 1968 to 1975, the number of homicides on annual basis roughly doubled, from 10,712 to 20,510. This means we were saving an estimated 50 guilty lives a year (the number we were executing as of 1960), but losing 10,000 additional innocent ones."

Licensed Crime

How many of those killings would have been deterred by swift, sure execution of killers? No one knows, but I agree with Van Den Haag who said, "The conclusion is inescapable that by making punishment as uncertain, rare and mild as we have, we have licensed crime."

The courts have gone to extremes in the protection of the felon's rights and have left the police tied up in red tape and ridiculous procedures. The results are obvious: thousands of killers walk out of the courtrooms thumbing their nose at the beleaguered police force. They know that "crime does pay." The risk of punishment must be too great a price for a felon to pay. He must say, "The rewards of the crime are not worth the risk of getting caught."

When a man is arrested for a killing, there is sorrow for the victim; for about 27 minutes. Then, the attention is focused on the criminal and the liberals cry, "He must be sick to have committed such a crime. Let's put him in a hospital for a while." So he goes to a hospital while the victim goes to the grave, but unlike the victim, the criminal does not stay put. A survey in Washington D.C. shows that 16 percent of all killers (judged to be insane) were back in society within five years.

My answer? If they are truly insane, lock 'em and leave 'em. If sane, try 'em and fry 'em.

Death Penalty Scriptural

As violent crimes multiply, capital punishment is being demanded by more people in this nation. There is no debate between knowledgeable people that it is scriptural. Foolish people point to the Bible verse, "Thou shalt not kill," as a reason not to have the death penalty. Even Sunday School pupils know that the Bible means, "Thou shalt commit no murder." There is a big difference in committing murder and killing.

I would not think of planning to take a person's life, but let a man kick down my front door, and I will shoot him without any remorse. You see, the protection of my home goes along with the honeymoon. I feel the same way about protecting my country in time of war. So, all killing is not murder and consequently not unscriptural.

In early civilizations, if someone killed your relative, you were expected to pursue him and seek vengeance by killing the killer. If he were rich, you could accept a cow, horse or sum of money to satisfy you. This was called "Blood Money" or "Payoff." There were many flaws in this system. A wealthy person could kill many people and pay off without any real loss to him. If the killer were a fierce warrior and he killed the father of a 9 year old child, there was not much chance of that child getting much justice. Then, Moses received a code of laws from God and put them into writing. From then on, it was up to the government to seek justice for everyone: rich and poor, weak and strong. This was a step in the direction of fairness and equal rights. God said, "an eye for an eye and a tooth for a tooth" and the government would extract the eye and the tooth. However, in recent years, the government has gotten out of the "eye and tooth extraction" business and civilization is falling apart as men no longer trust the government to protect them.

All Killers Not Deterred

Through the years, the death penalty has been used with more and less vigor and by many means. Various means, such as gas chamber, firing squad, electric chair, and decapitation, have been used. Regardless of how a person is executed, it is never pleasant for society or the criminal, and it was not meant to be.

The liberals tell us that we should not use the death penalty because it is not a deterrent. They present this argument so they can tear it down with ease. They seem to think that because they say this louder and louder and more and more, that it becomes a fact. They are "pulling on a rope of sand." They point to states that had the death penalty and also had an increase in killings. That does not prove the death penalty is not a deterrent. It only proves that all killers are not deterred. Nobody with any sense says that all killers are deterred. A person who is inflamed with hatred will not think about anything, so he kills.

If you are like most men, here is how you would react to your best friend stealing your wife: She runs away with your "friend" to Chicago. You think of buying a gun and going after them. If you were with them now you would kill them. You go out to buy a gun, but you start thinking about the electric chair. Then, you remember how your wife used to nag you. You think about how there are other fish in the sea. You think again about the chair; you don't buy the gun. Instead, you send a sympathy card to the man who took your wife!

Rehabilitation A Farce

We are told by the bleeding hearts that more poor people were executed for murder than rich people so capital punishment should be unconstitutional and not used in a civilized society.

Well, the accusation is true, but it is also true that more poor people kill than do rich people so more poor people should be executed. Rich people don't have the motives to kill since they have money, homes, and automobiles. They can travel anyplace in the world. They have numerous friends and associates. Usually, the motive behind a killing done by the rich is passion. Everyone, rich or poor, should be executed after a verdict of guilty by a jury.

The liberals tell us that an innocent man may be executed and his innocence discovered later when it is too late to correct the unjust sentence. There is that chance, but it is not likely with all the restrictions placed on the police, the emphasis on the rights of the accused, the jury trial, numerous appeals, and usually a long period on death row. Add to that the fact that most governors hand out pardons like campaign literature and are gutless "cry babies" who are super-sensitive to the bellowing and whining from the ACLU, NAACP, Urban League, and other radical groups who want almost everyone pardoned. It is interesting to know that half of the felons committing violent crimes should have been in jail. They were on probation, on parole or out on bail. Those who release these criminals must be held accountable.

Then, we are told that society must not execute felons because they may be rehabilitated while in prison. Well, that is not a valid argument if you believe God should be obeyed rather than unbelieving men. God said that a killer was to pay with his life.

The biggest joke in America is the "rehabilitation" program. Violent criminals are not being reformed by the prison system. Now, I am aware of the job being done in many prisons in leading men to faith in Christ and the change that follows in those lives. But that is not rehabilitation nor reformation; it is regeneration. That comes from God, not government.

I want to see as many non-killers helped as possible. I know men who have spent time in jail and have become productive citizens. I am pleased that men can continue their education while in jail, but rehabilitation is a farce. I see nothing wrong with admitting that law breakers should go to jail for two good reasons: to separate them from society and to punish them for their crime!

Capital punishment will not keep insane people and unthinking people from taking a life, but it will keep many criminals from using guns in robberies.

John D. Lofton, Jr. in the May 13, 1978, issue of **Human Events** reviewed Frank Carrington's **The Case for Capital Punishment: Neither Cruel Nor Unusual.** Lofton relates information taken by the Los Angeles Police Department in 1970 and 1971 from persons arrested for crimes of violence.

Felons Speak on Deterrence

Of the 99 criminals spoken to: "Almost 50 percent were deterred from carrying weapons or operative weapons by fear of capital punishment; Seven percent said they were unaffected by the death penalty because it was no longer being enforced; Ten percent said they were undeterred by capital punishment and would kill whether it was enforced or not, and thirty-two percent were unaffected by the death penalty, saying they would not carry a weapon in any event, primarily because they were afraid of injuring themselves or someone else.

"Thus, there was a 5-to-1 ratio of deterrance over non-deterrance as reported by those in the best position to make such a judgment: the criminals themselves."

Many of the felons that were questioned mentioned their fear of panicking during the commission of a crime and being "forced" to use their gun, thereby receiving the death penalty. So, they decided to leave their guns at home and not risk being burned. Now, only a mental midget says that is not a deterrent.

We will never know the thousands and thousands of men and women who sat in lonely rooms and decided not to kill their enemy because of fear of the electric chair. That is a deterrent. I say that we need to reinstate capital punishment and see that a killer gets a fair, fast trial and then on to the chair. How many killings will that execution prevent? I don't know but one thing is sure: The executed killer will never kill again.

March for Decency
Downtown Indianapolis, over 2,000 people

X

SHOULD TEACHERS, POLICEMEN, AND FIREMEN EVER STRIKE?

It is a crime for public employees to strike in most states and unwise to permit them to bargain collectively. According to Theodore Kheel, internationally famous labor mediator, "Collective bargaining and strikes are like Siamese twins." So, I am against collective bargaining in general and against strikes in particular for public employees.

Kansas City was ablaze during the fall of 1975 as firemen illegally struck against the taxpayers of that city. The 200 fires that erupted during the strike were contained by volunteers and the National Guard.

City officials accused the firemen's union of starting some of the fires. The volunteers discovered that the fire trucks had been tampered with, and oxygen had been replaced with carbon monoxide in an oxygen tank. The illegal strike ended after four terror-filled days.

Night of Fires

Memphis, Tennessee, saw a firefighters strike in July of 1978 with 350 fires in a couple of nights. The city officials accused some firemen of setting 90 percent of the 350 fires. Most arsonists go to jail for many years, but union members who torch buildings get a pay raise and more days off each year.

It was hot in Baltimore during July of 1974, but it got hotter: another illegal strike. It started with school teachers, then engulfed sanitation employees and then on to the firemen.

These "public servants" were then joined by the police, recreation department employees, and jail guards. The Baltimore strike was called by the American Federation of State, County and Municipal Employees Local.

Jerry Wurf, the International President, is reported to have said, "Baltimore City would burn to the ground" unless the city gave in to his demands. What incredible gall.

Unions at Their Worst

Dayton, Ohio, in August of 1977 was an example of public unions at their worst. During the three day strike at least 25 buildings burned and 30 families were left homeless. The firemen stood by and watched the homes go up in flames as the owners pleaded for them to do what firemen do best: extinguish fires. They refused.

A fire broke out at the Dayton Human Rehabilitation Center, a correction farm, and the inmates fought the fire because the firemen refused. One inmate said, "We got a sense of responsibility. What did they think we would do, just stand by and watch it burn like those firemen?" That inmate had more character than all the striking firemen put together.

One apartment house burned to the ground only three blocks from the firehouse. Two of the tenants escaped only with their pants. Three hundred and seventy-five firemen were walking the picket lines, some in sight of the fire. Pickets without principles.

City Caves In

The city caved in to their demands. When asked why the city capitulated, the president of the union said, "All he (the city manager) had to do was look out his window last night and see all those fires burning."

Also in the deal was total and complete amnesty for all firemen. Contempt of court charges were dropped. They should have fired the bums.

The charred homes are silent, smoking testimonials to the "professionalism" of the firemen's union. It is illegal to strike, but they strike anyway.

Police, firemen, sanitation workers, etc. are public employees. No one forced them to seek public service and nothing handcuffs them to public service.

They took an oath and did not keep it. They broke the law because they felt their cause was just. It's amazing how a man can adjust his principles to suit his position.

Wildcat Strikes

Many Christian men have asked my opinion on private sector and public sector strikes, and my position is very clear. I believe private sector employees have a right to strike if it is done legally. Wildcat strikes are always wrong, and a man of principle will not participate. He will cross the picket line and keep his commitment to his employer.

A picket line is not a barrier that keeps you out. It only tells the public that some workers are striking. You have every right to cross the line and work your job even though the loud mouths will call you scab, strike breaker and much worse.

No public employee should ever strike under any conditions. It will take courage when your co-workers are striking for you to do what is right and cross the line. Difficult? You bet. But who said life was a bed of roses anyway?

Gut-Rending Decision

Why should preachers and Christian school administrators be the ones who pay the price for their convictions and laymen never have to make a gut-rending decision? Christians and people with convictions will do what is right, not what is popular, pleasing or profitable.

When there is a strike in private industry, the public can usually go to a competitor. If your favorite frozen food company strikes, you can buy another brand or change to canned food. But what can a city do when the police force or firefighters strike? There is not another choice, so the public safety is threatened. The public suffers, and it is the public that pays the bills. The union and city officials sit down to bargain, but the public doesn't have much chance and taxpayers almost always lose their shirt.

Fine the Unions

Each state should pass laws that make it too costly for a public sector union to call a strike. A union should lose its dues deduction privileges for a period of a year and should be fined not less than a thousand dollars and not more than ten thousand dollars for each day of the violation.

Individuals who engage in a strike should be fined not less than one hundred dollars or more than five hundred dollars for each day of violation. It seems the law, oaths and responsibilities cannot keep some men from striking. Maybe the dollar will speak more loudly.

Last year, the Kokomo school teachers struck against the public and their students. Substitute teachers were in the classrooms and striking teachers asked if they were qualified to teach. I think the striking teachers proved **they** were not qualified to teach.

Moreover, 274 Indianapolis policemen drove their police cars downtown and parked them in the business area. Then, after turning on their flashing lights and sirens and locking their cars, they threw the keys into a trash barrel, thus making a long and tedious job of matching the right keys to the right cars. They tied up traffic as the citizens, who pay their salaries, tried to get home. Many of these men are my friends, but I am ashamed of their childish and ill-advised actions.

Unions Bankrupt New York

A perfect example of irresponsibility relating to collective bargaining and public union activity is New York City. New York City is not run by its elected officials but by power-mad union officials. New York also has collective bargaining and is completely controlled by the unions. The city is also broke. I seldom agree with the **New York Times,** but its July 8, 1975, editorial said, "New York is working for its unionized civil service workers, not vice versa. The real power in the city is held by the municipal unions."

The power needs to be in the hands of elected officials, not irresponsible union bosses. **New York** magazine gave credit to collective bargaining of municipal unions as one of the decisions that sent New York begging for funds and for suckers to buy their once highly rated bonds.

A sovereign government cannot grant to one special interest group (public employee unions) power and leverage that no other group can match. Congressman Philip Crane has asked, ". . . why should certain union leaders - of public employee unions responsible only to their own membership and utilizing pressure tactics that amount to blackmail, be able effectively to raise your tax rates - and those of your neighbor?"

State-Wide Strike

Power should not be in the hands of irresponsible union leaders like Gerald W. McEntee who is reported to have shouted, "Let's go out and close down this G.. D... state." And, out they went, and almost closed down Pennsylvania. Over 50,000 state workers refused to go to work: the first time in history that a statewide strike had been called.

The **Philadelphia Inquirer** commented on the union's actions in an unsigned editorial saying, "Is it healthy - is it tolerable - for a labor union of civil servants to be able to bring government, even partially, to a halt in pursuit of its members financial gains? Or in order to increase union leaders' power?" This question must be answered. Will the power to run a city or state rest in the hand of elected officials or in the sticky hands of union chiefs?

Lt. Governor Kline said of the Pennsylvania union officials: "The union leadership is the most irresponsible I have ever seen. People have been threatened and kept away from their jobs."

Those states now considering permitting their employees to form unions and bargain collectively against the public should consider the sorry record of public unions and collective bargaining when teachers, policemen, firefighters and garbage collectors stop work and illegally strike. So, if you like stinking garbage, store lootings, unrestrained crime, empty schoolhouses and a burning city, you will just love public sector collective bargaining.

Christian people in the work force and honorable non-Christians will keep their word and not strike against the unprotected public even if they sincerely believe they need more money.

Good Example

The police in Greenwood, Indiana, felt that they needed a raise; no doubt they did. They did the admirable and responsible thing and appeared before the city council and discussed the problem. According to a column in the Franklin **Daily Journal,** they were able "to reach a reasonable agreement" without hostility or threat of disruption.

The people of Greenwood are proud of the professionalism of their police department and the city officials who were sensitive to their needs. I trust others who work for the public will emulate the Greenwood Police Department and realize that a strike is immoral, illegal, short-sighted and a loaded gun to the head of the public.

Those foolish enough to strike may be foolish enough to look into the barrel of that loaded gun and pull the trigger just to see if it's loaded. A strike is a loaded gun, and it's dangerous to play with guns.

September 23, 1977

Mr. Frank Crane, Editor
THE INDIANAPOLIS STAR
307 North Pennsylvania Street
Indianapolis, Indiana 46204

Dear Mr. Crane:

This is to support the Star's position on striking teachers and to reply to Robert Thornberry, executive director of the Indiana Federation of Teachers.

Thornberry calls the teachers who were in the classrooms "scabs." Does he think the striking teachers were noble heroines? He said "parents have the right to know the truth." That's right; parents should know that striking teachers are law breakers. They are poor examples to young people who are more impressed with what they see than what they hear. He was very concerned about whether substitute teachers were qualified. Of course, a reasonable person questions the qualifications of the striking teachers. At least their character is in question.

Thornberry had the gall to say, "school officials were violating the law by using unqualified persons in the classrooms." Again, what does he think the striking teachers were doing? They were defying state law. They were saying, "we are above the law." They were telling their students, "obey the laws you agree with; disobey the rest." Parents also need to know that all teachers did not strike, even some who felt they needed more money. These were the professionals who put the interests of the students above their own. These deserve our support, the others our scorn.

Mr. Thornberry then tries to justify his untenable position by comparing the public sector to the private sector. He predicts victory for the public sector unions when they have a legal right to strike. If that happens, the state will be a loser and so will thousands of kids. I believe that even the teachers will lose since they will become more securely lodged in the vice-grip of the teachers' unions. They will help finance political candidates with their "confiscated dues," even if they oppose those candidates who dance to the tune of the union bosses.

Teachers, policemen and firemen should be paid an excellent salary. Their training and working conditions qualify them for good pay. However, they are public servants, and it is incredible that an intelligent man would compare public workers with the private sector. No one forced them to seek public service and nothing handcuffs them to public service. In striking, they break the law and a public trust because they think their cause is just. It is amazing how a person can adjust his principles to suit his immediate position.

Public sector employees who illegally strike should be given 24 hours to return to work. That will give those who acted in haste and heated emotion a chance to reconsider their illegal actions. If they refuse to return to work, they should be fired and stay fired. Taxpayers are weary of the arrogance of public employees who defy the law and have "sob-sister" judges lift contempt of court charges against them. We are weary of amnesty for them while FBI agents and those dedicated to national security are prosecuted and persecuted as criminals. Taxpayers are beginning to recognize public sector unions as public enemy number one.

A strike by public sector unions is a strike against the public. It is illegal, immoral, short-sighted and a loaded gun to the head of the taxpayers.

Sincerely,

Donald Boys
State Representative

DB / ld

October 26, 1977

Editor
THE INDIANAPOLIS STAR
307 North Pennsylvania Street
Indianapolis, Indiana 46206

To the editor:

I appreciate the good article on the editorial page of October 25th on "Child Molesters' Lib." It was excellent. However, today my main concern is a letter from Robert L. Thornberry, executive director of the Indiana Federation of Teachers. Mr. Thornberry calls me an employer of public employees since I am a State Representative. I consider myself an employee of the taxpayers of Indiana and more specifically, District 53.

Thornberry objects to my calling teachers, firemen and policemen, "public servants." I apologize for using the term. I thought it was a compliment. It used to be. He objects to my belief that any person working for the public be fired for striking if he doesn't return to work in 24 hours. True professionals who are guided by moral principles rather than by their union bosses will not break the law.

Thornberry then tries to play down a teachers' strike, saying that kids who have that experience will lose more time on fire drills than on strikes. Thornberry misses the point. We're not too concerned with the time lost, but the effect on kids who see their teachers breaking the law.

He then tries to put words in my mouth by saying I want teachers to "be a bunch of bootlicking public slaves . . ." No, I never even suggested that. But I would like to see thousands of "gutty" professional teachers stand up to the union bosses and get back to their job of teaching kids to read. His use of the word "slave" implies dungeons, chains, and torture. No public employee is forced to stay "chained" to his or her position. Teachers have the right to quit teaching and take a job in the private sector and work all year instead of nine months.

Thornberry assured us taxpayers that, "teachers do not want to strike." Of course, many teachers did not strike. Those teachers believe that what they are is as important as what they teach. Those that did strike did so of their own volition. They should also be willing to take their medicine. They expect their students to take theirs.

Notice that Thornberry did not address some basic questions raised by me. Namely, one, is it ever right for public employees to strike? Two, are striking teachers a good influence on their students? Three, how can he justify using teachers' dues for political activity?

If Thornberry will give me definitive answers to these three questions, I'll give him a grade of "C" on his report card even if I disagree with his answers. That will make up for the "F" he received for using "infer" when he should have used "imply" in his letter to the **Star**.

Sincerely,

Donald Boys
State Representative   DB / mr

XI

ARE RIGHT TO WORK LAWS GOOD OR BAD?

In a nation that puts a high premium on individual freedom, it is incredible that we must even debate "right-to-work" laws. Seventy-five per cent of Americans believe that unions should not have the power to force a person to join a union to acquire or keep a job.

Most Americans polled also believe a worker should not have to pay a fee to a union he chooses not to join. Over 60 per cent of union members also believe in "right-to-work" laws.

William Raspberry said, "If unionism is as good for workers as the unions claim, there should be no problems attracting members." This is an echo of what Samuel Gompers, the father of organized labor in America said many times: "Nobody should be forced to join a union. If the union serves its members honestly and fairly its members will come to it voluntarily."

But union bosses know their power and money will dissipate without the use of coercion. All unions are not corrupt and all union bosses are not little Caesars, but enough of the big ones are to smear the reputations of the others who are trying to do a good job for their members.

Unions Outside the Law

I believe the two primary functions of government are the protection of the innocent and the punishment of the guilty. Coercion and violence are a "no-no" unless perpetrated by the union bosses. The union bosses go free while anyone who gets in their way visits the undertaker. They seem to think they are outside the law.

Nobel Laureate, F.A. Hayek wrote about the unions saying, "they have become uniquely privileged institutions which the general rules of law do not apply." The unions feel that whatever they must do to accomplish their desires should be considered legal, even if they are obviously illegal.

Unions have done much for the working man in the last one hundred years, but they are doing much to him today. Some unions are a perfect example of a good thing gone bad.

We Needed Unions

One hundred years ago we needed unions to represent the workers to management in order to bring about much needed reform. But many unions think they are answerable to no one, not the states, not Congress, not the law or even to their own members.

Union bosses are among the most selfish, corrupt, insensitive, dictatorial and ruthless men in America. How did they get such a stranglehold on the nation and how do they maintain their grip?

One reason is the American people have been uninformed but that's changing. Another reason is that some members of Congress, governors and state legislators owe their political lives to union bosses. And, as one member of Congress said, "they don't waste an opportunity to repay the favor."

Any politician who dances to the tune played by any pressure group should incur the wrath of the electorate on election day whether he is a Republican or Democrat.

Workers Pay Tribute to Unions

I believe a worker should not have to pay tribute to an organization in order to keep his job. I believe in freedom from coercion. So do most Americans. Union bosses do not.

They are unsure of what they have to sell, and they prove it by forcing workers into the membership, confiscating their wages and calling it membership "dues." However, even non-members in most states must pay their "dues" and will be represented by union bosses whether they want to be represented or not.

What happens if a worker wants to represent himself or a small group of independent workers? Too bad; the union that he does not belong to will represent him anyway.

What if a worker does not want his "dues" going for political purposes that may be the opposite of his? Too bad; he has no option.

What if workers are religiously against the union and their activities? Too bad; religious convictions don't matter.

Freedom From Coercion

A "right to work" law would provide for the freedom of any

worker to join or refuse to join a union. He would not have to pay "dues" if he refused to join.

Union bosses who run their unions like two-bit Latin American dictators would not be thrilled with this freedom of choice for the workers. When a state considers freedom of choice the union bosses huff and puff and make all kinds of noise about how indispensable they are to the working man.

Some union bosses are angry with me because of my stand for freedom of choice of all workers in the private sector. If a man has the right to join a union, he must also have the right not to. One is not a right without the other.

Willis N. Zagrovich and Max F. Wright, president and secretary-treasurer of the Indiana AFL-CIO replied to an article I wrote on the "right to work," but they never answered the basic questions I raised.

The following questions can be answered very simply by union bosses: Do you believe a worker should be forced to join a union against his will? Or more simply, do you believe in coercion? Do you believe unions are sacrosanct and don't have to obey the law? Or more simply, should they be prosecuted for anti-trust violations?

Why did organized labor spend $8 million on liberal candidates in 1976 when most of the rank and file members are conservative? What option does a worker have if he does not want any of his dues going to a liberal candidate for public office? What option does a man have if he does not want the union to be his exclusive representative in labor negotiations?

Americans For Right to Work

Zagrovich and Wright did not like my statement that polls show 75 percent of Americans want "right-to-work" laws. They said, "there are reputable polls to show this statement to be inaccurate." What polls? When were they taken and by whom? The polls I referred to are Roper, Gallup and Opinion Research Corporation.

"Right to work" legislation will provide protection and freedom for unions and for the workers. It will release the strangle hold on the worker who is just a little reluctant to be choked to death. He will also no longer be forced to pay for the privilege of being choked!

My union critics want the government to guarantee a job to every person, but that is not the proper function of government. Government should provide the atmosphere that will produce jobs in a free enterprise system. If states lower taxes rather than raise them, they could attract more business into the state and provide more jobs and income.

How to Lower Taxes

We can lower taxes by forsaking our provider role and assuming a protector role. Get the crooks off welfare, and give more welfare to those who are deserving. Fire the lazy and incompetent state workers who think the state is their own private Santa Claus.

My two opponents said if Indiana continues to refuse workers the right-to-work, "it will attract new industry to our great state." Yes, business leaders will just rush into union controlled states to be pushed around by union bosses rather than go where there is freedom of choice. Zagrovich and Wright also believe in the Tooth Fairy.

It is interesting to note that it cost $9,000 more per year to live in Boston than in Austin, according to the Bureau of Labor Statistics. One reason is that Texas is a "right-to-work" state, while Massachusetts is not. Of the 20 states with the highest cost of living, not one was a "right-to-work" state!

Questions For Union Bosses

Zagrovich and Wright said that "right-to-work" legislation would mean a loss of jobs, and they may be right. A few union bosses may lose their "posh" jobs since they will no longer be permitted to turn the workers upside down and shake them by their heels and take their contributions to "feather their own nest." Maybe when union bosses have no money for political candidates, the reciprocal backscratching will stop - but don't hold your breath.

The union dictators don't want to answer questions about the rights of their workers; the rights of those who disagree; the violence; the raid on the pension funds; the sweetheart loans; political slush funds; and the general mismanagement of the various unions. But they are quick to tell you union members how kind, helpful and beneficent they are to the workers, and if you don't believe it, they will break both your legs and arms.

"Boys Cites Union Hoods and Strikes"
by Rep. Don Boys

Recently, UPI carried the story concerning Jacob Clayman, president of the Industrial Union Department, who has been appointed to head an investigation to discover why there is an increase in anti-union groups and increasing funds to conservative causes. Clayman said the results would be published, so "organized labor can compete with these opponents." Of course, Clayman is aware that conservatives are **giving** their money to defeat those political candidates who have sold their souls and votes to the union bosses. He is also aware that many unions must **confiscate** from the workers what is facetiously called "dues."

I can be a great help to Clayman's investigation and it won't cost the union bosses a dollar. First, Mr. Taxpayer is weary of those union leaders who think they are above the law. The law only applies to others according to some unscrupulous bosses. We are sick of seeing union violence, such as independent truckers having their coal trucks driven off the road and their coal dumped on the ground. We're weary of broken windows, slashed tires and union goons who run in packs like jackals. They are easy to identify since they have a streak of yellow up their backs.

Second, we are weary and rather embarrassed that we have so many judges and elected officials who deal more harshly with traffic offenders than with those who break criminal law. These are not immature teenagers who deserve a break. These hoods need to feel the full wrath of the law. If I treated my neighbor the way some union hoods treat non-union workers, I would be sent to the "slammer." Is there anyone out there who can explain the difference for me?

Third, a man who owns a business must be permitted to run that business and not have it run by a union. I will run my own business. My workers can strike if they desire; they have that right. However, if I can find replacements who will do an acceptable job for me, I have every right to hire those people, replacing those who chose to strike. Some misinformed people call that "scabbing." Most of us call it free enterprise Americanism.

Fourth, we're sick of those unionized employees who work for the public, i.e. teachers, policemen, firemen, etc., striking against the public in violation of state law. It becomes even worse when they try to justify their illegal and immoral behavior by constantly beating their breasts and weeping copious tears about their "sacrifice" for the public.

We are aware of the importance of their jobs and most people appreciate these teachers, policemen and firefighters. But, I wonder if they are aware of their own importance. They are too important to be permitted to strike. They were aware of this when they took the job. If they have changed their minds about striking, they should do the honorable thing and quit and go into the private sector.

Fifth, we're weary of these striking workers who are found in contempt of court yet never suffer any penalty. Elected officials show their lack of courage by caving in and making "no reprisals" a part of the settlement. The ringleaders should be fired, and they should stay fired. The public sector unions should be fined up to $10,000 per day for each strike day and their dues-withholding privileges should be withdrawn for at least a year. That way, they will have fewer dollars to spend on political candidates, and then maybe the legislative issues can be decided on merit rather than on what the union bosses want.

Sixth, we find it incredible that strikers receive food stamps. That forces us to support their strike against our convictions.

There are rumblings around various statehouses that collective bargaining is needed for public sector employees. But that will push each state to the brink of bankruptcy as in the instance of New York City. The **New York Times** said on July 8, 1975, "New York is working for its unionized civil service workers, not vice versa. The real power in the city is held by the municipal unions."

If you like stinking garbage, your city in flames, your streets unprotected, you will just love collective bargaining for public employees.

Of course, there are numerous unions and workers who are honest, efficient, law-abiding and who are making invaluable contributions to their state.

Informed people know there is a legitimate place for unions in our society, but that place is under the law, not above it. These are the good guys in white hats, while those breaking the law are bums wearing black hats.

So, Mr. Clayman, these are some of our grievances. The "our" translates "taxpayer," that forgotten individual who obeys the law even if it is a dumb law. He pays his taxes that are far too high and too numerous, and he only grumbles a little as he shells out his hard-earned dollars. He is a forgotten man, yet he is the most important man. He is a member of a union, yet he is not a member. He is rich, and he is poor. He lives in the country, and he lives in the city. He is even willing to freely give more dollars to elect conservatives to office who will listen to him and not to a union boss. He is Mr. Taxpayer, and he is for freedom and true equality, and you will rue the day you got him aroused by your union arrogance.

XII

SHOULD BLACKS RECEIVE SPECIAL PRIVILEGES?

If we were to change this chapter title to read, "Should Whites Receive Special Treatment," no reasonable person would concur; yet, leading Americans are demanding preferential treatment for blacks.

This nation should reward achievement and do its best to encourage ambition in every sector of life. But, there is a hue and cry from the "knee-jerk" liberals throughout the land to reward the under-qualified and under-achiever and to do so at the expense of the more qualified. I tend to believe that the hue and cry has been raised by those who have a vested interest in reverse discrimination.

Reverse discrimination is nothing more than discrimination of a member of a majority group to try to bring about equality. The long-term results may be equality, but it will be an equality of mediocrity.

Black Bigotry

The May 30, 1978 issue of **The Detroit News** quoted Detroit Mayor Coleman Young's candid statement on affirmative action: "The master and the slave cannot unite. It takes special steps to bring the slave up, then they can unite as equals . . . Some people say affirmative action is discrimination in reverse. You are d— — right, the only way to handle discrimination is to reverse it."

If the mayor appears to be a black bigot, at least he is an honest bigot. The mayor needs to be reminded that blacks are no longer slaves and have not been for over a hundred years.

Morally Blind

The Detroit News published an unsigned editorial saying, "Except for the morally blind, nobody doubts the plight of blacks nor the need for corrective steps. The question is: How can society remedy economic injustice in a constitutional manner and without creating a new injustice? To reverse the blade of discrimination and cut down whites, as blacks were cut down in the past, is retribution - not a solution."

I was challenged to a debate at Indiana University Purdue University in Indianapolis, Indiana on the subject of affirmative action. I debated Dr. William Marsh, professor of law at Indiana University Law School in Bloomington, Indiana and Reginald Bishop, a black columnist for the **Indianapolis News**. I asked Bishop how long America would have to give special treatment to blacks to atone for past discrimination of them. He answered, "two hundred years." Isn't it strange that I have been called a racist because I believe in equal treatment for everyone regardless of color and people like Bishop appear as champions of civil rights?

The Civil Rights Act of 1964 and subsequent Supreme Court rulings are supposed to guarantee that people would no longer be discriminated against because of race or color. Finally, the law would be color-blind. Questions on job applications indicating race and national origin were now illegal. Children would not be placed in schools according to color. This was supposed to be a major victory for all men and a giant step toward equality. From now on merit and ability would be the criteria for advancement.

False Assurance

Jeffrey Hart reminds us in his syndicated column that we were assured in 1964 by Senators Joseph Clark and Clifford Case that the 1964 Civil Rights Act would not result in reverse discrimination. Clark and Case were the floor managers for the bill when it came before the Senate.

The Senators issued a memo to legislators that, "Any deliberate attempt to maintain a racial balance, whatever such balance might be, would involve a violation of Title VII because maintaining such a balance would require an employer to hire or refuse to hire on the basis of race."

We were assured that there would be no enforced preferred treatment, but that was long ago and far away. The Fourteenth

Amendment to the U.S. Constitution guarantees equal protection under the law. But, it seems some people are more equal than others.

Special Treatment for Blacks

Along come the apostles of affirmative action, who tell us with a straight face, that since blacks have been discriminated against in the past, we need to suspend the normal meaning of the Constitution and give blacks special consideration to make up for past unlawful treatment.

We are told that blacks should not be admitted to colleges or given jobs using the same yardstick that is used to qualify white people for those positions. In other words, equal opportunity is not enough. Blacks must now have preferential treatment. We are told that the noble end justifies the distasteful means. However, that is not true.

To be consistent, these apostles of affirmative action should also demand that women be permitted to vote twice at each election since they were denied the vote until the Nineteenth Amendment. But then, the liberal is never concerned with consistency. In fact, the only thing consistent about the liberal is his inconsistency.

Patrick Buchanan wrote in **Human Events,** "Where the old discrimination, which favored white men, was odious and deplorable, the new is praise-worthy." Zing!

Notice we are not talking of a program that would identify the problem and seek to solve it by helping blacks enter the main stream of American life. We are talking about reverse discrimination and if discrimination is wrong, it is wrong for all people regardless of color.

White Wins Over Prejudice

This issue has been discussed and debated as it relates to Allan Bakke, a Vietnam veteran who applied to the University of California Medical School at Davis. Bakke was refused admission, not because he was unqualified, but because he is white. Bakke sued the university and the California Supreme Court agreed with Bakke. The university appealed the case to the U.S. Supreme Court that recently decided that Bakke was right and the medical school was wrong. Bakke has been admitted to the school.

The Court said that reverse discrimination was wrong but not too wrong. They said that race could be considered in college admission but could not be the determining factor.

The university reserved 16 out of 100 freshman spaces for minority candidates who failed to meet normal admission requirements based on testing and undergraduate grades. So, there was a two-track system at the university.

Those students seeking admission to the medical school were tested in four areas: verbal skills, quantitative skills, scientific skills, and general information. Bakke was superior in every area, except general information, although he was above average in that category.

Michael Novak wrote in the January 14, 1978 issue of **Human Events,** "In 1973, the year Bakke first applied for admission, the average scores of those admitted on the normal track were respectively: 81, 76, 83, and 69%. Bakke's scores were higher than average: 96, 94, 97, and 72. But the average scores of the minority candidates were: 46, 24, 35, and 33." So those students admitted on the lower track had scores that were less than half what Bakke had made, yet Bakke was refused admission!

Blatant Racism

Bakke's undergraduate grade average was 3.51 out of a possible 4.0. The average of students admitted without fair competition in 1974 was 2.62. It is also interesting to note that no disadvantaged whites have been admitted under this special program. Why not? If this is not blatant racism, what is it?

Such action is degrading and demeaning for all blacks. It implies that blacks cannot produce applicants who can score satisfactorily on the normal track in fair competition with everyone.

Grayson and Shepard wrote in **The Disaster Lobby,** "The proper way to eliminate inequities under which people were not hired or admitted to colleges because their skin was black, red, brown, or yellow, was to set up a system whereby people would not be hired or admitted to colleges because their skin was white." Wow!

It is not only unjust to whites who are not admitted, it is an unnecessary and unfair burden to place upon qualified blacks who may be falsely identified as "quota people."

The October 24, 1977 issue of the **U S News and World Report** said concerning reverse discrimination, "Whites and blacks alike might avoid using a black doctor, for example, in the mistaken belief he obtained his medical degree by meeting lower standards than those faced by whites."

Would it not be natural to be suspicious of a black architect you are considering to erect a skyscraper? Was he a quota person? Is he a qualified architect or is he second rate?

Liberals For Quotas

The reservation of a certain number of spots for a particular racial group is nothing more than a game called "Quotas Revisited." Most of us thought that we had progressed far beyond the day when colleges and businesses only permitted a certain number of blacks, Jews and women each year. But the same liberals that had condemned quotas in the past are now beating the drums and leading the parade for quotas in the present. What has changed other than the principles of the liberals?

"Quotas Revisited" received its impetus on August 22, 1971 when the **New York Times** magazine published an article by John Kenneth Galbraith of Harvard and two professors from Massachusetts Institute of Technology. It was called the "Galbraith Plan for Hiring the Minorities." It was pure quotas. The article said, "not merit, but sex, color, and ethnic origins would become the overriding considerations for hiring." And they have.

Liberal Senator George McGovern who is, in my opinion, a closet radical, led the Democratic Party Reform Commission in November of 1969 to adopt a series of resolutions that mandated the 1972 convention should consist of state delegations that contained specific quotas of blacks, women, and young people. After the Democratic Reform Commission adopted these unAmerican resolutions, McGovern told a reporter, "The way we got the quota thing through was by not using the word 'quota'." But liberals today are not as candid as McGovern. They don't use the word "quota" now. They call them goals and other code words that still translate, "quotas."

Full Steam Ahead

Eugene V. Rostow is a professor of law and former dean at Yale University Law School. In an interview with the **U S News and World Report,** October 3, 1977, he spoke on this subject of reverse discrimination. He said, "It is no kindness to anyone to put him into an environment where he's underqualified and where he will feel at a disadvantage and feel more stupid than he should feel."

Speaking of many minority candidates who drop out of college after meeting only a minimal admission standard, he said, "They are bitter, bruised and badly hurt by their experience." But what does that matter? Forget the irreparable harm done to blacks. Full steam ahead. The do-gooder will make poor doctors out of men who would make good bricklayers and average lawyers out of men who would make excellent teachers. Full steam ahead, roll over the constitutional rights of whites, and call it good and admirable. And when some soul dares question its fairness and legality, call him "racist!"

Jeffrey Hart said, "The proponents of racial discrimination scarcely bother to conceal what they're doing. Their demand is quite simply, that the constitution be changed in order to sanction what they wish to do. The rest of us cannot discriminate - but they can. That is the demand, one rule for them and another for the rest of Americans. This of course means no rule of law at all, merely the conveniences and taste of the reverse discriminators."

Carter for Reverse Discrimination

President Jimmy Carter, who speaks to hear the sound of his rhythmic voice, has spoken with a clear voice in favor of reverse discrimination. The **Spotlight,** a weekly paper out of Washington, reports in its January 16, 1978 edition that Carter will set aside 20% of the government's job vacancies exclusively for blacks and women.

The **Spotlight** article says, "the legislators and regular government workers also are concerned over the provisions of the new program whereby minority applicants would be exempt from having to take regular civil service examinations, and from having to compete against regular white applicants for government jobs. Instead, black and women applicants would be given a two-year trial that would then lead to permanent career civil service appointments (without tests) unless they are ruled undesirable for the position which in the circumstances seems very unlikely." America, the land of opportunity - if you are the proper color.

Liberals Don't Sacrifice

After we cut through all the rhetoric and clear away the smoke screen laid down by the politicians and liberal do-gooders, it comes down to this: reverse discrimination is the punishing of a job seeker or student applicant for an act of racism he did not commit and for an ethnic heritage over which he had no control.

The liberals are hanging the albatross of affirmative action around the neck of every black in this nation, qualified as well as unqualified. As the liberal does this, he whispers in the black man's ear, "I am your friend."

But the liberal do-gooder does not sacrifice. He does not surrender his privileged position, money and job so that an unqualified black can enter into the main stream. He is guilty of much sermonizing, but not sacrificing. The price for affirmative action will be paid by unsuspecting whites who were taught that all were equal before the law. They will soon learn that some are more equal than others.

A Black Speaks

Many members of minority groups detest and are ashamed of reverse discrimination. Dr. Thomas Sowell, a black economics professor at U.C.L.A., is among them. When Swarthmore College attempted to hire him under an affirmative action program, he replied: "Many a self-respecting black scholar would never accept an offer like this even if he might enjoy teaching at Swarthmore. When Bill Allen was department chairman at U.C.L.A., he violently refused to hire anyone on the basis of ethnic representation - and thereby made it possible for me to come there a year later with my head held up. Your approach tends to make the job unattractive to anyone who regards himself as a scholar or a man and thereby throws it open to opportunists." Sowell is a man of character and courage.

U.S. Government - Racist

Such an example of independence and character must cause the most vocal proponents of affirmative action to blush with shame. Affirmative action is pure racism and the biggest promoter of racism is the U.S. government.

Columnist Patrick Buchanan wrote in the January 28, 1978 issue of **Human Events,** "The U.S. government has become the paramount practitioner of racism in America. That seems a harsh thing to say, but is it not so? Who else requires the assignment of children to public schools on the basis of race? Who else imposes quotas for hiring based on sex and national origin upon college faculties? Who else commands federal contractors to engage in preferential treatment in the hiring and promotion of favored 'minorities'?

"The U.S. government - specifically, the civil rights divisions at

Justice and HEW, the 'contract compliance' crowd at Labor, and the EEOC does not see it that way. These civil rights zealots view themselves as angels of light to root out the vestiges of sexism and racism from American life. They are viewed otherwise, however, by their victims, the Italian, Irish, Jewish, Polish, Greek, Slovak and WASP teachers, professors, police and working men who pay for this federal altruism in delayed promotion and lost jobs see these bureaucrats not as heros, but oppressors."

Havoc in Schools

Affirmative action programs have created havoc in business and education. As a school administrator, it is my responsibility to find the most qualified person for a particular position regardless of sex, race or national origin. Any other basis for selection is not only discriminatory, but is a downward step in the quality of education.

Recently, this was experienced by a reporter who entered a third grade classroom of a black lady who was hired under federally ordered hiring quotas. The reporter pointed to a child and asked the teacher if she found him to be passive much of the day. The teacher only stared at the reporter. The question was repeated, "Do you find this child passive much of the time?" Again, no answer. The reporter then gently asked if she knew what the word "passive" meant? The teacher, a graduate of an illustrious Eastern college, admitted she did not know the meaning of the word!

The January 18, 1978 issue of **Review of the News** tells of a letter written by a black principal of an elementary school who was hired under federal quotas: "In the letter the principal consistently spelled the two letter word 'do' as 'dou'." Another administrator remarked, "after all we dou spell 'you' as y-o-u."

Incompetent Teachers

Louis E. Yavner, a member of the New York State Board of Regents, said, "There are teachers now being hired by, and presently working in, the New York City School System who do not know how to write a decent paragraph and would have trouble reading and understanding the daily newspaper." Many disadvantaged kids who need the most competent teachers will be saddled with these incompetent teachers.

Peter O'Brien, a former president of the school supervisors' union is quoted in the **New York Times** as saying, Hispanic teachers, "who could barely read or write English" had been made principals of schools "because traditional supervisory licensing examinations have been abolished as discriminatory."

Where will this lunacy end? Will blacks be given a pilot's license without a test because the exam is too tough? Will you ride with such a pilot? I suggest it is as criminal to put an incompetent teacher in the classroom as an incompetent pilot in the cockpit of a crowded 747.

Albert Shanker, president of the United Federation of Teachers, said concerning teachers who were unable to read or write, "We have lowered standards to a point where a significant number came in below the literacy line."

Admitting students to college on the basis of race or hiring and promoting because of race is as unreasonable as demanding that 80% of the players on college and professional basketball teams be white regardless of ability. Don't you think it is about time we accept people for what they are and not what color or sex they happen to be? I thought that is what America was all about.

Governor Bowen with the Author

XIII

IS THERE A RIGHT TO WELFARE?

Welfare is a monumental mess, a farce, a leech on the neck of this nation. Most people will agree that the sick and disabled should receive welfare, but women with five or six illegitimate children, receiving more money than a woman who cleans public buildings all night is preposterous.

It is common for "welfare queens" to pull up at your friendly supermarket in luxury cars and use free food stamps without shame. Speaking as one taxpayer, I object - strongly. I am weary of welfare people sleeping to 10:00 a.m. when I get up early to go to work. I am weary of them using food stamps for gourmet foods, wines and cigars.

I am weary of their demanding attitude. I don't owe the crooks, cheaters and career bums anything, and I believe it is the time to inform the politicians to clean up the welfare mess, or we will throw them out of office.

Welfare Immoral

Welfare is simply a mish-mash of government programs to take from the "haves" and give to the "have-nots." This thievery is justified by trying to "help the poor, the blind, and the disabled." It is nothing more than the redistribution of the national wealth. (Communist plot???) Anytime a man receives money he did not earn, there is another man who earned money he did not receive. That is immoral.

Since 1950 the number of welfare recipients has soared from 6,052,000 to almost 20,000,000 in 1978. In Newark, New Jersey one third of the population is on welfare! We are witnessing wildfire welfarism.

Henry Hazlitt said in **The Freeman,** May 1972 issue, concerning wild welfarism, "The causes of this accelerative increase are hardly mysterious. Once the premise has been accepted that 'the poor,' as such, have a 'right' to share in somebody else's income - regardless of the reasons why they are poor or others are better off - there is no logical stopping place in distributing money and favors to them, short of the point where this brings equality of income for all."

Right To Welfare

Hazlitt went on saying, "If I have a 'right' to a 'minimum income sufficient to live in decency' whether I am willing to work or not, why don't I also have a 'right' to just as much income as you have, regardless of whether you earn it and I don't? Once the premise is accepted that poverty is never the fault of the poor but the fault of 'society' (i.e., of the self-supporting), or of the 'capitalist system,' then there is no definable limit to be set on relief . . . the politicians who want to be elected or re-elected will compete with each other in proposing new 'welfare' programs."

But, of course, no one has a "right" to welfare. I believe I have a responsibility to help those less fortunate than myself, but they don't have a right to pressure me to take care of them. Those folk who talk of welfare people having a "right" to receive $12,000 to $15,000 per year from the taxpayers are not just plain folks but plain fools.

It is ironic but true that many families on welfare are better off than the families of those working men whose taxes provide welfare payments to the recipients! What about the rights of the workers?

Beginning of Welfare

How did we get in this welfare morass anyway? And, how do we get out? Welfare was originally handled by the churches and it was handled very well. James 1:27 says, *"Pure religion and undefiled, before God and the Father is this, to visit the fatherless and widows in their affliction . . ."* Note that this is the definition of pure religion not how to get it. So, the early Christian churches had an obligation to provide for the needs of the widows and orphans.

In the early days of the church, welfare became a minor problem as recorded in Acts 6. It seems the Greek widows were not being taken care of because verse one reveals they "were neglected in the daily ministration." The preachers called a meeting of all the Christian leaders and appointed deacons to care for the widows so the preachers would not get bogged down, "waiting on tables." The deacons were the first welfare directors! A deacon's job is simply to act as a servant to orphans and widows!

The churches in America were doing a good job providing for the less fortunate - alas, many lost their gospel message and began preaching a social gospel that helped the body but hampered the soul. Their emphasis was shifted from salvation to soup and men would no longer have an empty stomach.

The federal government was not very involved although local government was in some areas.

Government Inefficient

The federal government has proved to be not only insensitive to human needs, but it is also inefficient. Rus Walton, in his **One Nation - Under God,** gives a rule of thumb ratio between giving and receiving: "In person-to-person giving, a dollar given is a dollar received. In giving through voluntary organizations, twenty-five cents goes for administrative costs and seventy-five cents reaches the needy. Through state government, it costs one dollar to get another dollar to the beneficiary and through federal government, it takes almost three dollars to deliver one dollar. Caesar is a lousy steward!"

We should not be surprised that government does poorly with welfare; it does poorly in about everything it touches. It does do a good job producing red tape, bureaucracies, and mass confusion.

We don't do a man a favor if we do for him what he should do for himself if he is able. Booker T. Washington said, "In bestowing charity, the main consideration should be to help those who will help themselves."

This truth is beautifully illustrated in an ancient Chinese proverb that says, "If you give a man a fish, he will have a single meal. If you teach him how to fish, he will eat all his life." We should stop throwing fish to dead beats and hand them a spade to dig worms and a fishing pole to catch fish.

I am weary of the liberals who say that most of the welfare programs are humane, absolutely necessary and even Biblical. They are about as Biblical as a voodoo rooster plucking ceremony in Haiti. Something must be done about welfare in this nation.

Welfare Czar

There was little thought the federal government would

appoint a "welfare czar" until the depression in the 1930's. Factories were dark and silent. Men walked the streets looking for work. Once wealthy men sold apples on street corners. Bread lines were long and numerous. Rescue missions were filled each day. Those who could get gas money made their way out of the dust bowl, coal mines, and farmlands to California, Michigan, New York and other metropolitan areas.

The government decided to do something even if it was wrong. The United States would become a welfare state. We would start down the long road to socialism. We were told the new welfare programs would be temporary, but we developed a Frankenstein monster called the welfare industry. It was led by power hungry bureaucrats far from the people who fed the monster. The monster grew bigger and stronger, and it was in the self-interests of the bureaucrats to keep feeding the monster. Their future careers depended on more people qualifying for more and more welfare.

Helping people become independent and self-reliant was not good career planning. Those in the welfare industry produced a complex set of rules, regulations and exceptions, with the permission of Congress that makes it impossible to know what is going on at any one time.

There are 44 welfare programs, 29 being financed completely from federal funds and controlled by the "feds." In 1976 the federal government spent $187 billion for these programs, much of which was wasted since many of the 44 programs are overlapping.

Charles D. Hobbs says in **The Welfare Industry**, "Coincident with the extraordinary growth of welfare expenditures has been the development of a national welfare industry, now composed of 5 million public and private workers distributing payments and services to 50 million beneficiaries."

Tax Dollars Lost By HEW

Welfare expenditures are growing almost three times faster than the economy. It would be one thing if that money were going to the needy but much of it is wasted, lost, or stolen. The director of HEW admitted this year that his department is losing seven billion per year! He later corrected his figure saying only six billion was squandered or lost. I suppose he expects the harassed taxpayers to be grateful for small blessings.

The Associated Press reported on August 13, 1978 that HEW reported further losses for the first six months of 1978. They made, "only $146 million worth of errors in welfare payments to the aged, blind and disabled under the Supplemental Security Income program." Isn't that great? Only $146 million in errors in **one** of the 44 welfare programs!

The article went on to say that state and local governments administering Aid to Families with Dependent Children "misspent $441.2 million in a similar time period." Let's see, that's a total of $587.2 million that the two programs have "misspent" or lost in six months. Come on, you fellows can misspend more than that. You aren't even trying.

Rip-Offs

Very few Americans are aware of the numerous welfare schemes and "rip-offs" that take place. This is not to say that some needy people are not helped. They are, while others help themselves. It's Christmas all year long with Uncle Sam playing Santa Claus while sweating taxpayers fill his bag with goodies for the dead beats.

One of the most controversial federal rip-offs is the Comprehensive Employment and Training Assistance Program called CETA affectionately by the "rip-pers" (thieves) but called unprintable things by the "rip-pees" (taxpayers). The Department of Labor is supposed to be in control but, the program has been embroiled in controversy from the beginning, funding homosexual groups in many cities.

Tax Dollars For Gays

The August 14, 1978 issue of **The Spotlight** reported that the Gay Community Service of Los Angeles received more than $640,000 of your tax money to provide "education about gay lifestyles and gay people's problems." I suppose with $640,000 the most discouraged, dejected, and downhearted people would become "gay."

The article continued with more thrilling news: "The Gay Alliance of Rochester got $34,000 this year to provide speakers at local campuses to inform young people about homosexuality." It is bad enough that schools would permit admitted queers to have a public forum to flaunt their perversion but incredible that this "missionary" activity to college students be financed by tax dollars.

Those responsible for such irresponsible projects should be left hanging by their feet over the street outside their office buildings, destined forever to twist slowly in the wind. However, they will probably receive a government citation for "innovative planning" and may even be promoted to a position where they will have access to more government money (to translate: taxpayer's earnings).

New Wrinkle

New York City has added a new wrinkle to the old welfare racket with the cooperation of the state and federal governments. The generous city is restoring infertile welfare women to the condition where they can once again conceive! That's about as sensible as pouring gasoline on a fire.

The taxpayers are funding fertility restorations at a cost of 11 million (in New York City alone) and all women are included - married and single. There were over 2,000 fertility visits last year, but no checks were made to assure authorities that the women were even valid welfare patients or even if they were U.S. citizens!

It might be interesting to the "working stiff" to know that each "welfare child" costs the state (taxpayers) over $10,000 the **first** year. Oh, the joys of motherhood, courtesy of the beleaguered taxpayers.

Another federal program is the Financial Assistance For Higher Education. This program provides up to half of college expenses to students who have financial need. The money comes in the form of federal grants and federally issued loans. The dead beats who have defaulted on their college "loans" have cost you $400,000,000 while you have been struggling to send your own kids to college.

Then there is the Child Nutrition Program that provides "free" lunches and breakfasts to children in the public schools. (Of course, we know there is no such thing as a free lunch or breakfast). Some families must pay a small fee for the meals depending on their income. However **all** children in "areas of economic need" receive free summer meals regardless of income!

Kids Dump Free Meals

I have spent the last five months on a special select committee investigating various welfare programs funded by the "feds" but administered by the state. My committee visited a public school unannounced while breakfast was being served. We watched well dressed, healthy students take the reduced and free meals. We also watched them throw the half-eaten meals into a garbage can and pour their milk into a bucket.

Who could be critical of kids being fed breakfast before starting the school day? I can if the parents are too lazy to get out of bed and act like parents. I can if parents drop off their kids early so they can get to work. I can if the parents are collecting Aid to Dependent Children and food stamps. But then I am a monster since I don't believe in 95% of the welfare schemes.

The remainder of the 44 programs provide for food stamps; feeding the elderly in senior citizen centers; medical care for women, infants, and children; loans to rural families to purchase homes; loans to urban dwellers to purchase homes; and rent subsidies up to 70% of fair market rental value.

Now to the "biggies": Medicaid provides almost all medical costs for low-income families; Medicare provides subsidized hospital care for the elderly and disabled and has just decided to pay for sex change operations at a cost of $5,600 for a San Diego man! Social Security Old Age and Survivors Insurance provides monthly payments to retired workers; and Social Security Disability Insurance pays monthly benefits to disabled workers.

Most of the 44 programs are expanding at a rapid rate and all overlap into other programs. It seems the left hand doesn't know what the right hand is doing - or doesn't care.

Get Rich on Welfare

Charles D. Hobbs presents a humorous theoretical family on welfare in **The Welfare Industry:** "Here, for example is a family of eight which could theoretically qualify for 39 programs. It consists of an alcoholic Indian veteran in job training and going to college who lives in New York City with his 75 year-old retired father, his 60 year-old work-disabled mother, his disabled coal miner brother now on sick leave from a railroad job, his recently unemployed sister-in-law, and his mentally retarded Cuban refugee wife and their three children, one an infant hemophiliac, one a ten-year-old junkie, and one a teen-aged school drop-out. If such a family exists, it could become wealthy on welfare."

The above "family" does not exist but many similar families do and are taking the taxpayers for a ride. There are thousands of "welfare queens" living high and relatively safe from detection because of indifference, inefficiency, and incompetency of the welfare industry. But, what does it matter, the federal welfare bag is without a bottom.

There must be a stopping place somewhere or the day will soon arrive when more people will be getting handouts than are working to provide the handouts. I suggest we tell the elected officials to clean up the welfare mess or we will throw everyone out of office. We will no longer accept stalling, supine excuses, self-righteous justifications, or high-sounding double talk. We demand a change - now.

Workers and Shirkers

A change is coming, but it means more payments and more people qualifying for those excessive payments. A **guaranteed income** is in the offing in the near future if the politicians have their way. Each American family would receive cash payments depending on the size of the family. Rich and poor would be paid the same amount if family size is the same!

Then, there is the negative income tax that takes from workers with higher incomes and gives to those at a lower income level.

We won't even discuss the morality of taking from the workers and giving to the shirkers. Let's talk of what it will do for those who have little character and self-respect. Some of them will cut back their working hours to 20 or 30 hours per week or better yet (for them), they will stop working depending on how the give away finally functions.

A recent report of an experiment by HEW carried out in Seattle and Denver proves the above contention. William Raspberry, a black columnist writing in the November 23, 1978 **Indianapolis Star** commented on the experiment: ". . . when people were given guaranteed income and also allowed to keep a significant portion of what they could earn by working, they worked less."

Welfare People Not Fools

Martin Anderson asks in his **Welfare: The Political Economy of Welfare Reform in the U.S.:** "Why should someone work 40 hours a week 50 weeks a year for, say, $8,000, when it would be possible not to work at all for, say, $6,000?" He says that people on welfare may be poor but they are not fools. That's right, the fools are bureaucrats and elected officials who devise and approve such unproductive, unAmerican, unfair, and unworkable schemes.

Ronald Reagan said in the May 6, 1978 issue of **Human Events** concerning Carter's proposed welfare plan that it "would give welfare benefits, including earned-income tax credits, to nearly 12 million families earning between $10-15,000 a year and to four million families with incomes between $15,000-25,000!" It pays to be poor!

Is There a Right to Welfare?

It has been suggested that a guaranteed income might wipe out all other 44 welfare programs and could be administered by the IRS thereby gutting the state welfare agencies as well as HEW! Well, if we must have a guaranteed income (and we don't), the negative approach with the destruction of all other programs is preferable. That's like giving a man a choice of being hanged or shot with the victim paying for the bullet or rope!

Reform the System

Welfare has made our cities a time bomb. Something must be done before they explode. I have some suggested reforms for the welfare racket:

1. Inform state and federal welfare bureaucrats that the plan is to cut **back** on payments, not increase them. The ideal is to make people self-supporting, not dependent on federal or state largesse.

2. All able-bodied recipients must perform some public service to qualify for any welfare. If he refuses, let him not eat! Paul, the apostle, told the Thessalonians, "if any would not work, neither should he eat." It won't be long before they start to work.

3. When a recipient gets a job or has an income, his welfare stops. If he refuses a job because it is "demeaning," he should lose all benefits. Of course, no one on strike should receive **any** welfare.

4. Welfare recipients should not be permitted to vote until they are self supporting. It is insane to permit welfare people to help put men in office who promise more and more welfare payments. Isn't that buying and selling votes? I remind you that the vote used to be restricted to property owners so my suggestion is not so unthinkable.

5. Reduce the welfare workers by eliminating most of the programs.

6. Simplify the welfare industry. It is so complex, no one seems to know what is going on. We need to "put a handle" on the entire welfare program.

7. Cheaters should be prosecuted to the fullest extent of the law. Thievery is still thievery.

8. Every piece of legislation should include an "impact statement" as to the effect on wealth redistribution. That would permit legislators to know the true ramifications of each proposed bill and permit them to vote against any bill that would expand welfare.

9. Surplus foods, such as inexpensive soy beans, could be used to feed welfare recipients. It would be nutritious and keep them alive,

but they would get the message that they would eat much better if they went to work.

10. Maybe the government could shame the churches into doing what is basically a church responsibility: helping the widows and orphans. The Mormon church is the only church I know that is doing this as a matter of policy. What about the rest of those who claim to be Bible oriented churches? Have they decided that this teaching is not for this dispensation? Very convenient.

The Welfare Bomb

That ticking you hear is the welfare bomb that will explode someday, tearing out the soul of this great nation. Some brave, selfless, conscientious, politician needs to defuse the bomb. If he gets the job done, he will become an authentic American hero that parents will tell their children about in hushed, reverent tones and whose story will be sung in truck stops and bars across the land; "He killed the welfare industry."

And if he fails? He will be defeated at the polls, killed politically by a coalition of union bosses, welfare functionaries, welfare recipients, and bleeding hearts. Is there a politician out there who will take the chance of becoming a hero or a zero? Is there anyone who aspires to be not a politician but a statesman? I hope so; our future depends on his ability and determination to disarm the welfare bomb.

I suggest we provide for the needy and prosecute the greedy.

XIV

GRASS: TO BE WALKED ON OR SMOKED?

Grass should be walked on, but never smoked. This succinctly expresses my view on marijuana. I'm aware that the trend seems to be against this philosophy, but I have never followed trends. I find they keep changing.

Surely if marijuana can be proven harmful, no responsible person would advocate its decriminalization. Well, guess what I am going to try to do. If I can convince just one young person not to smoke marijuana, then this book has been worthwhile.

Harold M. Voth, M.D. is a member of the staff at the Menninger Foundation and is Associate Chief of Pyschiatry for Education at the Topeka Veterans Hospital. Dr. Voth said in a speech delivered before the Rotary Club of Kansas City on September 30, 1976, "Make no mistake, marijuana contains a very toxic substance. Its regular usage favors retrogression, flight, and apathy - the very last kind of human qualities people need in these uncertain times."

Marijuana Harms Cells

Dr. Gabriel G. Nahas has a medical degree and has earned his Ph.D. from the University of Minnesota. He is a professor of anesthesiology at Columbia University in New York City. He has written 400 scientific articles and is a member of 15 professional societies. He is also a consultant to the United Nations Commission on Narcotics. When he speaks on the subject of drugs and their effects, people listen.

In the November 1977 issue of the educational journal **Listen**, he gave an interview on the subject of marijuana and its effects on the body. It is a blockbuster. Dr. Nahas said one reason marijuana is harmful is because it is retained by the body for a long time. He said, "It takes a week before a single dose is completely eliminated from the body." Marijuana has a cumulative effect, and "has the potential for harming the cells."

Nahas says that marijuana harms the cells that divide, and points to the white blood cells that protect the body against disease. Grass smokers lose protection against disease because their cells do not divide rapidly and cannot destroy invading foreign bodies. The doctor continued, "If these young men have children, there is a danger of genetic damage to the offspring."

According to laboratory observations, marijuana is more harmful to women, because a female has only 400,000 germ cells at birth, while a man manufactures sperm cells daily. He said, "Every germ cell that is impaired will remain imperfect." He added that with the males, "There is a large instance of abnormal sperm cells."

Dr. Nahas said it is possible, "A destructive effect of marijuana on offspring might appear only after several generations." Obviously, a responsible person would go very slow when it comes to changing the laws on marijuana since there are reputable specialists that tell us it is not an innocent "pleasure drug."

Changes the Brain

According to the interview, the most obvious characteristic of marijuana is that it changes the brain. The brain will "remember" as it is imprinted with a chemical memory. This imprint is usually associated with a feeling of pleasure, which "induces the desire" to smoke more marijuana. That would indicate addiction!

Nahas further says that marijuana will produce "subtle alterations . . . (which) might include, for instance, minimal brain dysfunction." A drawing accompanied the article that illustrates what marijuana does to the brain. Drawing "A" was done at 7:30 p.m., just before marijuana was given to a subject. The drawing was one of a man's figure done well. Drawing "B" was drawn by the same person at 9:25 p.m., after the dosage had taken effect. Drawing "B" is nothing more than so much scratching. I think that is a devastating argument against the use of marijuana and its legalization.

Ann Landers and Pot Smoker

The following letter was sent to Ann Landers by a pot smoker to prove how harmless pot is and how lucid the smokers of marijuana are. Notice the spelling, grammar and obviously confused mind of the writer:

Dear Ann Landers:

Your letter against pot last week was a joke. If you dryed up creeps want kids to believe you, who don't tell the truth? I like my hair long. It looks fine. I have yet to see a single letter in your column tell the GOOD things about pot. Why is that? Because you are a bunch of fuddy-dudies who are scare us kids to death. Well, it won't work. Most of us know more about pot than our parents and teachers put together.

Getting turned on by Jesus is definately. I'm a 16 year-old girl who lives in a medium-size midwestern town. I have been smoking pot at least once a day for two years. It hasn't hurt me at all. In fax it has done me a lot of good. Not only is pot-smoking fun but it has expanded my conscientiousness and opened my eyes to the beaties of the world and unquestionable. This proves the police are pigs.

Grass has not dulled my mind. It has sharpen it. My think is clearer than it ever was. I am more aware things I never noticed before. Objicts that used to look small look large, especialy when I. When I smoke, I see mental images in color instead of black and white.

I used to be too shye to speak up in a crowd. Now I am a brilliant conversationist. I get stoned yet I am 100 percent lucid. I am express my inmost feelings brilliantly. Feet can be friends. When I finish this letter it will be a mastpiece.

If you fail to print it, I will know you are a Communist. In Russia they print only one side of story. The side they want people to believe. I'll be watch and waiting.

The Truth Will Win

Dear Truth:

Your letter in the unedited form proved that a person who is stoned is no judge of his lucidity, his brilliance or the caliber of his performance. I should have printed it au natural the first time.

So a person is not in control of his mind after an average dose of marijuana.

Open Door to Hard Drugs

Dr. Nahas observes that marijuana is an open door to other

drugs. He revealed a study done at Columbia University, involving 5,500 New York State high school students. The study was published in **Science** (December 1975) and "clearly states that marijuana is a crucial stepping-stone toward the use of heroin or other dangerous drugs."

The study showed that among students that were heavy users of marijuana, "26% went on to use heroin or other destructive drugs." The kicker is that only 1% of students that were not marijuana smokers ended up on heroin! So, if you don't smoke marijuana, you have a 1% chance of getting on heroin, while your odds are 26% if you smoke pot.

Marijuana then, is not an innocent weed. One would have to be hard up for thrills to smoke it in light of the abundant evidence as to its debilitating effects. The **New York Times** reports: "In Colorado, some mine operators report that marijuana smoking on the job is beginning to rival alcohol as an occupational safety hazard."

Stan Evans reported in his **Indianapolis News** column on December 26, 1977, "A six-month sampling of persons stopped for erratic driving by the California Highway Patrol disclosed that roughly one in four showed blood samples containing tetrahydrocannabinol, the active component of marijuana." A very high "one" may be driving toward you and your family tomorrow on the highway.

Damaging to Unborn

The July 30, 1978 issue of the **Indianapolis Star** published a front page article by Peggy Mann headed: "Tests Show Marijuana Damaging To Unborn." Robert L. DuPont, former Director of the National Institute on Drug Abuse, was quoted as saying, "I get a very sick feeling in the pit of my stomach when I hear talk about marijuana being safe. Marijuana is a very powerful agent which is affecting the body in very many ways."

The article continued, "The full range of these consequences (of using marijuana) is now starting to come clear. At the medical school of this historic city (Reims, France) last weekend, 41 scientists from 13 nations presented new research findings linking the use of marijuana with harmful effects on human reproduction, the brain and other body cells, including the lungs."

But the most chilling effect was on the innocent unborn children. The researchers, represented by Prof. H. Tuchmann-Suplessis of Paris University, who is a world expert in birth defects said, "that marijuana, though not producing deformed babies, was fatal to the unborn."

It is good to know that marijuana will not deform babies, although we have had testimony that future generations will be affected. But, marijuana will kill unborn babies!

Why then the big push to legalize marijuana if it is so dangerous to the smoker and to society? But no, the push is to "decriminalize" it, not legalize it or so the story goes. Whatever you call it, the results will be the same; more marijuana smoked by more people.

White House and Drugs

There is another result of legalizing marijuana, according to Dr. Nahas. He said, "Once marijuana is taken out of the category of a forbidden drug, there will be pressure to free others." (cocaine, heroin, etc.)

This pressure is even coming from the White House. Dr. Peter Bourne was President Carter's advisor and maker of drug policy until he was pressured out of the job for breaking the drug laws! The **Catholic Register** quotes Bourne as saying, "There is no doubt that marijuana will be decriminalized in a few years. I'd like to see NORML (a pro-pot organization) switch its energies to working for lesser penalties for possession of other drugs." The **Register** article says Bourne looks with favor on "an experimental heroin maintenance program," with the taxpayers providing free heroin at government clinics.

So, the White House not withstanding, experts testified that grass will damage the brain, lessen chances to throw off diseases, will affect future generations, build up a dependency for more marijuana, open the door to hard drugs and can kill the unborn. That's why I say: walk on the grass, or even cut it, but never smoke it!

Brownstown Rally
for Religious Freedom

XV

DO THE CULTISTS HAVE RIGHTS?

I'm a fundamentalist. I have no love for weird cults and the Eastern religions that have become very popular. But I believe those people have a constitutional right to preach their weird doctrines. I don't like to see them confuse the minds of people and indoctrinate young people, but they have that right. If the false religions don't have that right, then the day will come when the government will say that you and I don't have a right to exist and propagate what we believe.

I'm concerned about the restrictions that are being put upon the Moonies and others, because I know if government can restrict them, they can restrict me. However, whenever they break the law, they should go to jail or pay the penalty.

Bills were introduced in at least nine state legislatures in recent years calling for investigations into tax exempt status of various religions, their solicitation practices and whether they employ mind control techniques. Others are demanding an investigation of the cults and all "unapproved" religious groups in the wake of the Jonestown tragedy.

Charlatan Preacher

There is no doubt that the bizarre happenings in the jungle of Guyana is reprehensible and deplorable; however we must not be stampeded into doing something that future generations will curse us for doing.

James Jones was, in my opinion, a charlatan. He was a Communist who in his last years did not believe the Bible. He used it as a tool. James started his ministry in Indianapolis, Indiana, and after a faltering start in the ministry as a Disciple of Christ preacher, he started the Peoples Temple. He specialized in faith healing, racial integration, social services to the needy and finally developed a domineering posture over his followers.

He became convinced that Indiana was "too racist" and moved to California in 1965 with 100 of his subjects. He developed a large following in San Francisco and even became friendly with the leading politicians as he had done in Indianapolis. He returned to the Peoples Temple a few times and told his Indiana followers that in his San Francisco Church, "no one dies."

Into The Jungle

However, he lost his enthusiasm for California and negotiated a lease with Guyana for 27,000 acres of jungle land to start a commune that he named "Jonestown." Over 1,000 people, mostly blacks, sold everything, gave the money to Jones and followed the self-annointed "Prophet of God" to the "promised land."

People appeared to be happy in Jonestown as the village was developed, but stories seeped back to California that: the people were virtual slaves; bizarre sex offenses were encouraged; Jones had a mistress and children by other women; Jones also had some male "friends;" and that there were people who wanted to return home but were kept as prisoners.

Murder at the Airport

Word reached Congressman Leo Ryan (D-Calif.) of the problems in the jungle community, and he took a crew of 20 to visit Jonestown to investigate the charges. He saw the smiling faces, the church, the school and appeared to be convinced that the stories were unfounded. However, as he and his group started to leave, a few of Jones' disenchanted followers left with him. Jones saw his empire crumbling beneath him.

While the Congressman's group was boarding the planes, Jones' followers shot and killed Ryan and 4 of his people. It was all over, even Jones knew that. He called his followers together and had cyanide laced Kool-Aid passed out to all. Children had it sprayed into their mouths. Bodies started dropping within minutes and after five minutes, all were dead.

Mass Suicide

Jones died with a bullet in his brain and around the commune lay over 900 bodies of his followers. Jones, who had boasted in Indiana that none of his San Francisco followers had died, had led them to mass suicide. The singing has stopped in Jonestown; the Bible, used as a tool to control people, lies closed on the pulpit; the tabernacle is silent and empty; and above Jones' throne on the platform swings a sign in the jungle breeze, "He who does not learn from history is doomed to repeat it."

The "Prophet of God" did not learn from history or from the Bible he professed in his early days to believe! A Bible verse that Jones read and preached many times says, "Whatsoever a man soweth, that shall he also reap." (Galations 6:7) As his bloated body lay decaying under the hot sun, it was a silent testimonial to the truths of the Bible.

As horrendous as this incident was, we must not over-react. Jones should have been investigated for fraud, mismanagement of funds, etc. but not for religious activity. The government has no authority to decide what is "acceptable" or "unacceptable" as it relates to religion. Those convicted of crimes can and should be prosecuted, but religious convictions must be untouched by government.

Restrict Freedom of Religion

Representative John Culbreath of Florida wants to investigate religions he doesn't like. He said, "I want to find out what's going on with these organizations . . . In these cults, they actually demand panhandling, and they're annoying." He went on to say, "in true religions, people give time and money voluntarily." Well, I'd say to the Representative from Florida that the cultists may be annoying, but they have a constitutional right to teach and preach what they believe, and if they're "annoying," that is part of the price we have to pay to live in a free nation.

Culbreath's resolution called for a committee to study problems caused by religious cults. Well, it's the Moonies today and the Methodists tomorrow or the Baptists. Some are concerned about the recruiting techniques and about illegal indoctrination methods, but if they can restrict these people from teaching and propagating, they can also keep Christians from handing out literature on the street.

I would not be unhappy if the cultists would all leave the country. It would thrill me, but I am concerned if a state can close down one religious group, they can close down another. You can't put restrictions on one religion simply because you disagree with them. Surely, we've learned that in this nation.

Our Heritage

We often talk of our American heritage, but we can not be proud of the religious restrictions placed on people who did not believe as the majority did. Our ancestors fled persecution in Europe to gain religious freedom and upon their arrival, they persecuted those who disagreed with them!

Some colonies made church attendance compulsory while the Maryland Constitution gave the legislature authority to tax the population for "the support of the Christian religion." The New Hampshire Constitution made the same provision.

The early American colonists believed that Indians had few rights since they were pagans. Some thought they were serving God by taking the Indians' land away from them!

Maryland, settled by Catholics, permitted religious freedom to all except Jews and Unitarians while Plymouth restricted only Quakers. Roger Williams, the Baptist, was booted out of Massachusetts Bay Colony because he spoke out for separation of church and state. The authorities also frowned on his criticism of their punishing people who "broke the Sabbath." Williams is known as the father of religious liberty and no treatise on freedom of religion is complete without looking at his life.

Seeds of Truth

He was born in London and, while still a boy, met one of England's greatest lawyers, Sir Edward Coke. Coke was helpful to Williams while he was being educated at Cambridge. Coke was a contemporary and friend of Thomas Helwys, who, like Coke, opposed King James on the divine right of kings.

Sir Edward probably was responsible for planting in young Williams the seeds of truth relating to the individual worth of every human soul regardless of social, economic, or educational status.

Williams was ordained in the Church of England following an outstanding college career that resulted in his receiving a degree in 1627. But the Church of England was too stiff for Williams, and he became a Puritan followed by a decision to become a Separatist.

The seeds of religious freedom, planted by Sir Edward Coke years earlier, had blossomed to fruition and led Williams and his wife to leave England and seek his ideal in a new land far from his native England - Boston in America!

Voted For Oppression

The Pilgrims had landed at Plymouth in 1620 having left England because of religious oppression. The Puritans followed a few years later. The Pilgrims wanted complete separation from the Church of England while the Puritans only wanted to clean up the Church; especially the trappings left over from the Roman Catholic Church. The two groups got together and formed the Congregational Church which was to be supported by the taxpayers! They had risked their lives and all their worldly goods crossing the Atlantic to find freedom of religion and when they found it, they voted for oppression instead of freedom. They were no longer on the outside looking in; they were the "in group" and they liked it.

Sunday Laws Oppressive

Williams came to Massachusetts and found there, as in England, a religious monopoly. He didn't like it and told the church leaders why he opposed them. They weren't accustomed to such opposition and were indignant at such audacity. But, the common people heard him gladly. He told them their Sunday laws were oppressive and contrary to liberty and personal dignity. He told them if the authorities could tell a man he had to go to church, they could also tell him he could not attend church. He suggested that each person should decide for himself what he believed and when to attend church; and personally stand before God and take the consequences.

He fled Boston for Salem and then to Plymouth where he stayed two years learning the ways and language of the Indians. He was convinced that the Indians should be paid for the land taken by the white man, and he preached this to the consternation of those in authority.

Williams was banished from the colony by the governor but was permitted to stay until his health improved and until the birth of his daughter whom he named, Freeborne. But he continued to preach until an order was issued to arrest him and ship him back to England. However, Williams escaped with a small group in 1636 and went to the land of the Narragansetts.

They stopped at a spring of water and after rest and meditation, Roger called the place, Providence. They were home. The Indians were paid for the land and Rhode Island soon became known as a haven for religious freedom.

First Baptist in New World

Williams became convinced that only believers in Christ should be baptized and since babies cannot believe, he refused to baptize them. He organized the first Baptist Church in America in March of 1639 near the fresh water spring called Providence.

The Rhode Island charter, procured from King Charles II was a miracle document espousing freedom of religion and personal responsibility. It is especially astounding since King Charles II was one of the most vociferous persecutors of the Separatists.

The Charter provides, "That no person within the said colony, at any time hereafter, shall be anywise molested, punished, disquieted, or called in question for any difference in opinion in matters of religion which do not actually disturb the civil peace of said colony; but that all and every person and persons may from time to time, and at all times hereafter, freely and fully have and enjoy his and their own judgments and consciences in matters of religious commitments."

Rhode Island became a beacon of light, leading harassed people to a colony where freedom of expression and freedom with responsibility were a pleasant reality. But Rhode Island was unique in the New World.

Convert Them or Kill Them

Unlike Rhode Island, New York, New Jersey, North Carolina, Vermont and others excluded Catholics from holding any state office. The Massachusetts Body of Liberties (1641) gave authority to civil courts to try those who "worship any other god, but the Lord God." The punishment? "He shall be put to death." In other words, "if you can't convert 'em, kill 'em."

As one religious conservative, I believe a man can believe what he wants to believe, and it is not any of the government's business. However, if his belief is translated into illegal actions, he must be stopped. ("Beating the devil" out of children; handling snakes in the presence of children; "Worshipping God" by going nude on a bus.) But, I must vigorously defend the right of all to believe and worship as they desire even if it offends me. If any group can be restricted, then I can be restricted, so I must fight for the rights of everyone in my own self defense.

I believe the liberals would love to pass laws prohibiting church members from going on visitation and "annoying" people by knocking on their doors and inviting them to Christ and to church. Even though we don't agree with these other religions, we had better be quick to defend their right to exist because our freedom will be threatened next.

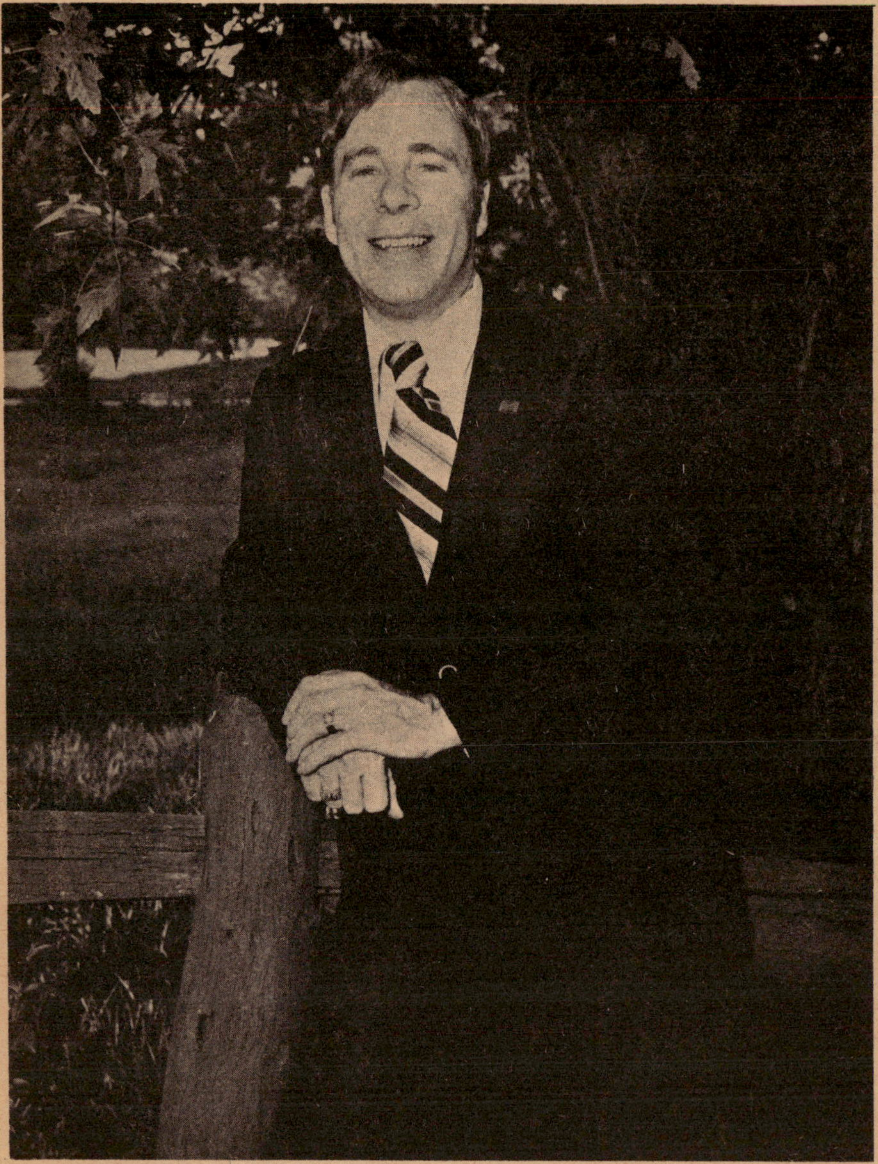

XVI

OUR AFRICAN POLICY: REASONABLE OR TREASONABLE?

America has been a nation of "good guys" who stood for the weak, helpless, and crippled peoples. We have been the selfless defender of freedom and the foe of tyranny. We have emptied our coffers and spent the blood of our finest young men in the cause of liberty. We have, at times, reacted to bad advice and made unfortunate decisions that were counter-productive to freedom; but then, we never professed perfection.

However, we are now pursuing a path in Africa that is bringing reproach to the red, white, and blue. We are not being faithful to those Americans who lie in shallow graves in Korea, the South Sea Islands, Vietnam, France, and Germany. Our friends are puzzled and our foes are delighted. There is no defense or justification for our position on Africa. We are wrong. We have lined up on the side of the Communists, and when the lights go out in Africa, it will be the U.S. who pulled the plug.

Black Killers

We have sided with bloody Marxists who have: blown a civilian airplane out of the sky and slaughtered the 18 survivors; butchered numerous innocent missionaries; raped helpless little girls; forced civilians to cook and eat their own ears; kidnapped children to be trained as terrorists; slaughtered ranchers; bombed buses of civilians; murdered Red Cross personnel; planted landmines on highways, killing innocent blacks and whites; shelled cities, killing women and children; and numerous other acts of terrorism that are taking 30 lives per day, 90% of them black.

Former Secretary of State Henry Kissinger said, "the Carter

Administration is seeking to encourage the most radical of the terrorists and has no concern whatsoever for the white minorities."

A case in point: Russia wants to control the Red Sea and the Horn of Africa. Somalia and Ethiopia lie on the East Coast of the continent. Russia chose to support Ethiopia in its war with Somalia by pouring arms and supplies into Addis Ababa. Somalia officials requested aid from the U.S. to counter-balance the build-up in Soviet Ethiopia, but Carter refused their request with the hypocritical reply: "African problems should be solved by Africans themselves."

What he meant was: We will not use American tax dollars to help a nation in its valiant fight for freedom against overwhelming odds, but we will use our clout, money, and prestige to drive Rhodesia to its knees and force South Africa to adopt our ideas of tolerance.

Our Biggest Mistake

Our biggest mistake in Africa revolves around Rhodesia and South Africa, our two oldest and best friends. But, then, in recent years we have been guilty of kicking our friends and kissing our foes so our present policy is standard operating procedure. We are spitting into the wind.

Rhodesia is a nation of 268,000 whites and over 6 million blacks. The whites are farmers, professionals, miners, shop owners, and soldiers. The blacks run the gamut from stone-age bushmen to the well-to-do. The white controlled government broke away from Britain in 1966 and is considered illegitimate by the United Nations. The UN doesn't like their treatment of blacks.

Sixty per cent of the Rhodesian Army is black. Responsible blacks can vote, stay in any hotel, eat in any restaurant, and attend any church. How long has that been true in America?

Economist Milton Friedman, after a trip to Rhodesia said, "Rhodesian blacks in the modern sector enjoy an average income that is considerably more than twice as high as that of all the rest of Africa."

Rhodesia, now called Zimbabwe Rhodesia, has been ruled by an elected parliament consisting of 100 members, 20 of them black. Prime Minister Ian Smith had two black cabinet members. But the liberals demanded more. The U.S. has interjected itself into the internal affairs of Rhodesia to force its will on them. When did we get that right? The same liberals that are demanding interference by the U.S. in Rhodesia are the same ones who screamed and demonstrated because we were helping South Vietnam after an official request for help.

Submit to Black Rule

We are told that Rhodesia must submit to majority rule-black rule. Every black must be permitted to vote; one man, one vote. An analogy would be if King George III had told the American Colonists that they must submit to majority rule of the Indians. Would any sane people willingly vote for their own destruction?

Liberals make much of the fact that 200,000 Rhodesian whites dominate the lives of over 6 million blacks, yet the reverse will be true after majority rule. Is that more reasonable? The whites will flee or be driven out of the land they developed and the government will be run by untutored blacks with only a handful of knowledgeable leaders. Of course, a black dictatorship is preferred to a white democracy! Is that reasonable or treasonable?

It is interesting to note that in the nations where the whites are a majority, there is much talk of minority rights; however, where the whites are the minority, there is no clamor for minority rights. Is this not racism? Is there any clamor for majority rule in Britain's Crown Colony of Hong Kong? Why not? If majority rule is good for the blacks in Rhodesia and South Africa then it is good for the Chinese in Hong Kong.

Majority Rule in Russia

If the U.S. must attack a racist country, why not try Russia? Is there majority rule there? How about Red China? Why are the bleeding hearts not weeping copious tears over these nations who deserve our tears? Are all politicians hypocrites, or do hypocrites become politicians?

Another example of hypocrisy is our relationship with Nigeria. Nigeria is a military dictatorship without any freedom. They have public executions. They have black leaders and black gold-oil. The U.S. needs oil, so Nigeria is "respectable." Has anyone out there heard any demands by the U.S. that Nigeria clean up its act and restore human rights? The silence from the White House is deafening.

There are 43 independent states in Africa that are controlled by dictators, military juntas, and a president-for-life. Most of them are run by black Communists and the U.S. is friendly to them, yet

Britain and the U.S. are demanding that the anti-Communist South African and Rhodesian governments be run to satisfy the liberals.

Internal Solution

The United Nations and others have been telling Rhodesian leaders that black rule was inevitable, and they should accept it even if it means the loss of the white man's freedom. They finally agreed and planned to have a new Constitution by December of 1978 that would provide for 72 black members of parliament and only 28 white members. All blacks, 18 years of age, would be permitted to vote under this new "internal solution." Well, now the radicals would be satisfied. Not quite. In the national election where 64.5 percent of the voting population voted, Bishop Abel Muzorewa was elected Prime Minister, but the international busybodies are still not satisfied!

The U.S. has insisted that two Marxist terrorist groups be a part of that plan! We got what we wanted-then blew it. The two black rebels have insisted that their terrorist armies that have been looting, killing and raping the whites and blacks of Rhodesia be the mainstay of the police and military of the new Zimbabwe!

Converted Communists

Have the Communists been converted? Don't they still plan to bury all free people? Is Carter surrounded by fools or traitors or both? Do not informed people know that coalition governments with Communists don't work? If Carter thinks the Communists can be trusted, what has led him to that conclusion? Is Carter so naive to believe that a black Africa will leave the Russian camp and rush to the open arms of the U.S. because we "chopped off the legs" of our friends in southern Africa?

Are we supporting the Marxist terrorists because it will please the Communist countries in Africa and will win points with uninformed black voters in the U.S.? Is Carter more concerned over the election in 1980 than the freedom and safety of the peoples of southern Africa?

Charming Butchers

Just who are these men the U.S. and Britain want to be a part of the new Rhodesian government? None other than Mugabe and Nkomo, the "Bobbsey Twins." Mugabe is a Mozambique-based terrorist leader of ZANU who was afraid of the "internal solution" because, like Nkomo, he knew he couldn't win in a free election. He wants all 7 million Rhodesians turned over to him, and he will produce a one party state colored not black, but Red. Newsweek March 20, 1978) asked him, "Do you consider yourself a Marxist?" He answered, "Yes, I do." He has promised to execute Muzorewa, Sithole, Chirau and Smith!

Joseph Nkomo is the leader of ZAPU and operates out of Zambia. He told the **Rhodesian Herald,** (July 1977) "Let me tell you, it (Rhodesia) will be a socialist state." His official organ, **Zimbabwe Review,** is printed in Communist East Germany. Nkomo told **Time** (Aug. 1977), "The British know the right thing to do. Smith is a rebel, and they should do what they did in America-line the rebels up against the wall and shoot them." Can you imagine the outcry from the liberals if this statement had been made by an anti-Communist dictator friendly toward the U.S.? These are the two rebels that Carter wants to be a part of the new government.

At his press conference on March 9, 1978, President Carter called those two charming butchers, Mugabe and Nkomo, the "Freedom Force leaders outside of Rhodesia." He said that they must be involved in any peace settlement. Doesn't he know that they were invited repeatedly to participate in the "internal solution" but refused? Surely Carter knows it is no longer a white-versus-black issue in Rhodesia but a struggle among various blacks for leadership.

Control of Minerals

The Communists are not interested in majority rule nor are they concerned over the living conditions of the blacks. World dominion is the name of the game. They want to control the raw materials and keep them from the free world. Rhodesia sits on top of two thirds of the chrome of the world and chrome is essential in the production of steel. Russia gets much of her chrome from Rhodesia. The U.S. has been buying chrome from Russia at twice the price because we didn't like the way Smith ran the government. We won't buy, at reasonable prices, from Rhodesia who happens to be our friend. Instead, we buy from Russia our avowed enemy!

If the U.S. is cut off from chromite ore, our steel and space industry will suffer. Men will be out of work. Prices will rise. All this because the Administration wants to force a freedom-loving people to their knees. Is this reasonable or treasonable?

Choking on Bone

The Republic of South Africa is another bone in the Administration's throat; one they may choke on. South Africa has 5% of the total population of Africa and only 4% of its land mass, yet is responsible for over 25% of Africa's gross national product and 20% of its agricultural output. (Only 25% of the 4% land mass of South Africa is arable). They must be doing something right.

The Republic of South Africa is a nation of 4.3 million whites and over 20 million blacks. According to the Jan. 1978 issue of **Government Executive,** "the 20 million blacks include some 5 million Zulus; 4.8 million Xhosa; 2 million Tswana; 800,000 Shangoan; 750,000 Indians and other Asians; 2.5-3 million Coloreds'; . . . 600,000 Swazi; 500,000 Venda, and about 600,000 'others'. Many have a bitter distrust of each other, the result of murderous blood-feuds going back centuries."

Tribe Not Race

What many critics of South Africa have not understood is that tribe is far more important than race. Liberals try to make the racial conditions in the U.S. analogous to South Africa, and in doing so, they are "pulling on a rope of sand." The blacks in South Africa are not descendent from slaves, and there is more hatred among the various tribes than between the whites and blacks.

Here in the U.S., we all speak the same language and have the same general religion, but in South Africa there are seven different nationalities of blacks, each with their own language and religion. If all the tribes and religions of South Africa are melted into one nation, what language would be taught in the government schools?

It seems to be far more reasonable to follow their present plan: that of providing separate homelands with each tribe electing its own parliament, speaking its own language, running its own schools, and living according to its own customs.

It is not true, as some have asserted, that the whites callously took the land from the blacks hundreds of years ago and systematically excluded and oppressed the blacks as the whites developed their own culture and civilization. The facts are that whites, neither British or Dutch, have ever moved into the black areas of South Africa.

Southern Africa Settled

The Dutch were expanding their empire and landed at the Cape of Good Hope on April 6, 1652 to open a rest station for their ships returning from the East loaded with treasures. The crews would rest, the ships would be supplied with rations, and the homeward journey would be completed. There was no intention to colonize, however, farmers started arriving and built farms along the First River. So, South Africa was born, and others soon came to the Cape. The second group to arrive was a large group of French Huguenots.

It was 1795 that the British arrived and took the Cape from the Dutch. The Germans followed in 1857. The only blacks in the area at the time of the Dutch arrival was a small group of Hottentots who were almost decimated by a smallpox epidemic. The Dutch, after losing the Cape to the British, moved almost 500 miles north and formed their own nation. They are known today as Afrikaners.

Today, the two basic white groups are British and Dutch (Afrikaner) who live together rather well, as one nation. The Parliament meets in Cape Town in deference to the Dutch while the Executive branch is located in Pretoria in deference to the British. Until recently, the government has been led by John Vorster (pronounced Foster). The new prime minister is Pieter W. Botha who has taken the same political position as Vorster.

Apartheid Not All Bad

The white government of South Africa has pursued a policy of separate development (called apartheid by their critics) for whites and blacks. They plan to give the blacks their independence in their own tribal homelands. Transkei has already been set up for over 3 million Xhosa-speaking blacks and Bophuthatswana for over 2 million of the Tswanas tribe.

South Africa has also controlled South West Africa since the League of Nations mandate of 1920. South West Africa is 4 times as large as Britain with a population of 852,000 consisting of 11 tribes. After independence, it will be renamed Namibia.

The most vocal criticism of the white government in South Africa has revolved around its laws dealing with the blacks. Until recently, all blacks had to carry "Pass-books" and show them on demand. There were also laws forbidding inter-racial marriage, now repealed. These laws were designed to keep the races separate and distinct entities in keeping with their policy of separate development.

Apartheid is not good, but it is not all bad. It is easy for us to criticize the South Africans at a safe distance of 12,000 miles for their treatment of a unique problem. Many of the 200 laws covering apartheid deal with education and economics that protect blacks from unfair white dominance and competition. Of course the South African critics never discuss that facet of apartheid.

Speaking of Money

It is also not mentioned that 10% of the taxpayers (whites) contribute about 70% of the total national income. In the last 5 years, the real wage of the average black worker has increased more than 30% while the average wage of the white worker has not increased at all.

In 1977, the overall income of whites dropped 4% and blacks' income rose by 11%. Medical care costs the blacks from one dollar to $15.00 with the top being $50.00 for a heart valve operation that would cost $15,000 in New York.

Soweto the Slum

The western press has made much of the rioting in Soweto, a mostly black suburb of Johannesburg. The uninformed call Soweto a slum; a slum that has 300 churches, 279 schools, a 3000 bed hospital, 11 post offices, 8 clinics, 63 nursery schools, 1600 black-owned firms, and 50,000 autos with one third of them being the luxury, Mercedes-Benz. Those 50,000 autos roll over Soweto's streets, 75% of them paved.

They have athletic events in their large facilities: one stadium seating 50,000 people, another over 12,000. There are plans to build one to seat 100,000 people. Well, the people in that "slum" lived far better than I did as a boy. In my town, we didn't have a stadium, a paved street in front of our house, a hospital in the whole county, a nursery school, and not one Mercedes-Benz! I didn't know until now that I was so deprived.

South Africa is building in Mitchell's Plain near Cape Town, a modern housing development for 250,000 blacks, financed by the white workers. So, conditions are not as bad as some liberals tell us they are and probably not as good as some South African politicians say they are.

Conditions Not So Bad

If conditions are so bad for blacks then why has the government not been forced to build a wall around the country with properly spaced gun towers to keep oppressed blacks from fleeing? The fact is, the blacks have it better in South Africa than anyplace in Africa. Thousands of South African workers are citizens in neighboring countries ruled by black tyrants. They work in South African mines and are paid in gold for their work. The problem is that so many want to come to South Africa because of the good working conditions, housing, and medical care.

But the radicals in the U.S. and Britain demand a change in the government to give that nation, admittedly built by whites, over to the blacks. To hear some critics talk, there is no freedom in South Africa for blacks, so a change must be made - now!

They demand a change in the 300 year-old nation. They will not accept a gradual implimentation of black rule in the homelands to protect the rights and lives of the whites.

An old South African proverb says, "slowly over the rocks." This phrase goes back to the Afrikaner pioneer days when they slowly lowered their wagons down rocky and steep hillsides to arrive at their settlements. Too much haste and they would be dashed to pieces on the jagged rocks below. I have a suspicion that the U.S. desires a "smashing on the rocks" of the South African government. And remember, that government is our friend and also anti-Communist. Again, is that reasonable or treasonable?

Liberals' Double Standard

It does not seem to distress the liberals in our government that 90% of the African nations are ruled by one party or military regimes: that 90% restrict the press, free elections, and personal rights. It does not seem to disturb them that blacks can not vote in pro-Communist black nations like Zambia, Mozambique, Tanzania, Angola, Uganda, Botswana, and Ethiopia. The U.S. is not threatening these nations but then, it's our friends we kick in the teeth.

The U.S. cut off the sale of arms to South Africa in 1963 as well as spare parts, yet we are helping the bloody regime of Vietnam through the World Bank and are even talking of foreign aid (tax dollars) to them! We are even going to sell jet planes to Red China if the President gets his way. The widows and orphans of those Americans slain in Korea and Vietnam would not call that reasonable but treasonable.

Nation of Producers

South Africa, under white leadership, has built a nation of producers that has benefited white and black citizens. They produce more than 70% of all the gold produced in the western world and about 50% of all the gem diamonds of the world are produced in South Africa and South West Africa. South Africa is also the largest producer of platinum in the free world.

The Republic of South Africa and Rhodesia hold 96% of the free world's chromium resources and South Africa has over 25% of the western world's uranium resources. Other minerals in abundance include coal, asbestos, nickel, iron ore, and manganese. The U.S. must have manganese to produce steel.

America imports over 100 strategic minerals from South Africa. How can we be so cavalier about the future of South Africa when we are tied so closely to them? It is not melodramatic to say that our future is dependent on the freedom light burning brightly in South Africa. Yet, the windbag liberals are trying to blow out that light.

Eighty of the world's top minerologists met in Mbabane, capital of Swaziland in 1976. Those experts concluded that the Soviet Union's primary interest in southern Africa is to deprive the industralized west of its supply of crucial minerals, thus causing severe disruptions of the free world's economy.

Ready for War

Remember, South Africa can get along without us, but we can't continue on our same standard of living without them. They produce 75% of their military needs including jet fighters. They are prepared to stand alone if necessary. They have stored at least 2 years supply of oil in abandoned gold mines. They have an army of 41,000, a navy of 5,500 and air force of 8,500. They have a Citizens Force of 165,000. Add to that the 35,000 South African Police comprising 19,000 whites and 16,000 blacks. These are well-trained, well-armed men ready for war.

They also have the capabilities to produce a nuclear bomb! They appear to be ready to defend their nation against the international do-gooders, busy-bodies, and carping critics like Andy Young, Jimmy Carter, and Britain's David Owen.

According to the **U.S. News and World Report** for Nov. 21, 1977, "the defence budget rose 40% in 1976 and jumped another 21 per cent this year, to nearly 2 billion dollars." They have been getting ready for years. They will not turn over their nation to uneducated, pro-Communist blacks without a fight. Can any reasonable person blame them?

When Lights Go Out

The U.S. not only has a vital interest in South Africa because of their resources but because of their geographical location. The southern tip of the nation, called the Cape of Good Hope, juts into the Atlantic and Indian Oceans. Each year, 24,000 ships, mostly tankers, sail around the Cape carrying 80% of Europe's oil supply and 50% of America's.

Our nation must have access to the sea lanes around the Cape since our giant oil tankers cannot travel through the Suez Canal. If we can't get oil via the Canal or from around the Cape, the U.S. will be forced out of the foreign oil markets. When our lights go out, and we sit in our dark, cold homes, there will be little comfort from the noble human rights speeches delivered by Carter.

When will our politicians learn that the U.S. should make decisions based on the interests of the U.S. and not on world opinion? We don't have to approve all that goes on in South Africa, Rhodesia, South Korea, Argentina, Chile, or the Philippines, but we must consider our own national security.

A Question for Liberals

Why are liberals selectively indignant? Why does the U.S. insist on forcing our views on those nations friendly toward us and remain strangly silent and helpless about the slaughter in Cambodia, the Cuban involvement in Africa, and the demise of human rights in Red China and Russia? It is one thing for us to be an international bully but to bully our friends and buddy-up to the international gangsters is inconsistent and insane.

Chinese and Russian vessels ply the Indian Ocean and find a welcome in the ports of the black Communist nations while the U.S. has **rejected** a South African offer for us to use freely the naval base at Simonstown! Is it not in our own interest and the interests of the free world to have a friendly port at one of the most strategic spots in the world? We could have a base to monitor all Soviet ships skirting the Cape; we could have an anti-submarine base there; and we could refuel our ships without sending tankers all the way to the Indian Ocean as we are presently doing. We refused the South African offer of the free use of a safe harbor! WHY?

When the government is friendly toward us and wants to make a contribution toward freedom, why are the liberals clamoring for embargoes, divesture, and the dismantling of the friendly white government? Are those liberals racists?

Storm of Hate

The March, 1978 issue of **Government Executive** said, "Some of the outfits raising this storm of hate and violence in South Africa are well-remembered by Americans from the 1960's. Among these: the Southern Christian Leadership Conference, American's for Democratic Action, American Friends Service Committee . . . the Ford Foundation . . . the Carnegie Endowment for International Peace . . . the U.S. Catholic Conference; World Council of Churches to Combat Racism." And on and on.

So, what happens if the liberals in the U.N., Britain, and the U.S. have their way and southern Africa falls into anarchy and finally lands in the Communist camp? What will Andy Young do then? Yell at Cuba? Stop smoking Havana cigars? Cry on the steps of the U.N.? Use Venezuela sugar in his Chinese tea instead of Cuban sugar? Maybe he will lead a company of marines on Red Square. Or, maybe he will just stomp his feet in a pique of anger. Whatever he does, black Africa will still be Red and enslaved.

None Dare Call It Treason

When the Rhodesian and South African economies grind to a halt under the leadership of the black Reds; when the treasuries have been raided and the funds stored safely in Swiss banks; when crops rot in the fields and inoperable tractors stand idle; when the phones, johns, elevators, and trains refuse to work; when the large firms have been nationalized; when whites have fled both countries or have been butchered in Mau-Mau type uprisings; and when the dream of black rule has turned into a nightmare, will the gloating radicals in our government finally be satisfied? And, like China in the late 1940's, Korea in the 1950's, and Vietnam in the 1960's, none will dare call it treason.

XVII

BARBS BY BOYS

Following is a series of hard-hitting newspaper columns, letters, and speeches by the author.

CARTER ATTACKS THE CHURCHES!
by Don Boys (R-Greenwood)

"My first project . . . will be to wipe out the right wing." So said Morris Dees, Jimmy Carter's fund raiser and general counsel for the Committee for Jimmy Carter. This threat was made just after Carter's election as King, rather, President of these United States.

It is not surprising to many informed people that those who are religiously conservative are also politically conservative. So, if Jimmy, "I will never lie to you," Carter can scuttle the churches, Christian schools, missionary societies, and religious radio and TV broadcasts, he will at the same time wipe out a major source of opposition to his Frankenstein schemes.

Thinking conservatives oppose his schemes, whether they come through legislation or royal edicts that would mean more deficit spending, more welfare, higher taxes, international cowardice, abortion, ERA, treating perverts as normal people, interference in internal affairs of other nations, gun control, and federal intrusion into business and personal lives.

Theological conservatives make up a block of over fifty million people, plus other millions in the old line churches. We Christians are getting more vocal and active, and isn't it strange that we are also having more problems with various departments of government? Maybe it is only a coincidence. Yes, and if you believe that, you also believe in Santa Claus, the Easter Bunny, and the Tooth Fairy. I also have some oil stock you may be interested in.

If Christian conservatives don't become informed and get involved in their federal and state governments, they will be living and serving Christ in the "catacombs" sooner than anyone expected.

One of the most ominous and most serious threats to all religious, educational, scientific, and medical groups is **House Resolution 41**, that has already passed a House sub-committee and is now before the House Post Office and Civil Service Committee.

Representative Charles Wilson, Democrat from California, introduced House Resolution 41, which will regulate all charitable institutions that seek contributions by mail. All these groups will be inundated with mountains of red tape and federal forms that will demand the most confidential information; information that is absolutely no business of Uncle Snoop.

Religious leaders will spend great amounts of time and money detailing the purposes of their churches, schools, broadcasts, etc. and the exact use to which they will put the solicited money. The Post Office could confiscate corporate records to "verify" their statements. Then, the church's confidential list of contributors would become public information under the Freedom of Information Act. If religious and educational leaders are not subservient enough to the unelected bureaucrats, the Post Office officials could order a mail stop on the organization and the cash flow would cease, and so would the ministry.

Churches, schools, radio and TV broadcasts, and camps must have money to operate. No money, no ministry. No ministry, no influence on the voters, and no influence on the nation. What did King Carter's man say? "My first project . . . will be to wipe out the right wing." But he will use a multi-pronged attack.

The Post Office Department has not had the experience that the IRS has had in terrorizing the American people. They are experts at terror. They cannot operate without it. They have forgotten they are servants of the people. The IRS has become a Frankenstein monster that feeds on the uninformed, the gullible, meek, and the weak.

The March-April issue of **Freedom Line,** edited by Dr. Paul Cates, published a certified letter sent by the IRS to a fundamental church in Atlanta, Georgia. The letter was to be answered in thirty days, and was accompanied by two extensive questionnaires for the church and their Christian School.

The IRS wanted to know if the church was accountable to any other organization. They asked, "Does your organization have a recognized creed and form of worship? If so, please explain in detail." (Most questions were to be explained in detail.) The church answered by saying, "Recognized by whom? Please explain in detail."

Another query was, "Does your organization impose a formal code or doctrine upon its members?" And, another was, "Does your organization require renunciation of any or all former religious beliefs on the part of your members?" Can someone tell me what business that is of the IRS?

Further questions dealt with the church's ecclesiastical government, the church's "religious history," and the ordination of its ministers. They wanted to know what qualified a man to be a minister, and wanted a "copy of their Certificates of Ordination that had been issued to them." Is the IRS going to decide the qualifications of ministers?

The IRS asked if the church had "a regular congregation or regular religious services, if so, please give frequency and average attendance. Also state where these services are held i.e., a church, a residence, other?" The church asked what the service meant by a "regular" congregation. Who decides what is regular or irregular?

Uncle Snoop wanted to know how many church members they had, and, if any applicants for membership had been rejected, and if so, why? They also asked for membership requirements! They also asked, "if any applicant had been turned down for membership?" How would the IRS accept the news that many churches have refused membership to unrepented adulterers, drunks, and perverts? My, my, my, what grist for the mills of the hypocrites of the ACLU and other radical groups.

Then these servants of the people wanted to know if the church had any Sunday Schools for the young. Question 23 wanted a "complete list of your officers and directors including a brief resume of their background. . ." Then into the master computer!

Question 24 demanded: "identify those contributors who have given $500 or more during the most recent accounting year." The following question wanted a detailed accounting of receipts and expenditures for the recent year.

It is my opinion that any religious or educational leader who provides such information has sawdust in his head. Maybe the IRS should be reminded of the First Amendment to the U.S. Constitution: "Congress shall make no law respecting an establishment of religion or prohibiting the free exercise thereof. . ."

The Atlanta church asked the IRS, "Does the IRS have the authority to define a church, integrated auxilaries, worship, or religion?" I submit to you that when government, Congress, the courts, or anyone has the right to decide what is an "approved" religion, this nation is on its way down the tubes.

Churches, schools, and private individuals should keep proper records and be businesslike in all affairs, but they should not be intimidated by petty county, state, and federal funtionaries. We should each remember to ask these officials questions like: "Why must I do that," or "What is your authority," and we should demand that it be "put in writing in detail within 30 days." We should be firm without being arrogant. And, as always, we should be Christian in all our dealings with men and government entities.

It might be wise for us to take the offense when we are being harassed by government officials. There are state and federal statutes to protect us. The U.S. Criminal Code, Title XVIII, Section 241 says, "If two or more persons conspire to injure, oppress, threaten, or intimidate any citizen in the free exercise or enjoyment of any right or privilege secured to him by the Constitution or laws by the United States or because of his having exercised the same . . . they shall be fined no more than $5,000 or imprisoned not more than 10 years or both." Maybe we should slap a suit on any Post Office official or IRS agent who harasses or intimidates us. That would take some of the enthusiasm out of their work, and might eliminate some of their terrorist activities.

We must remember that government was given to us by God for our good, but God did not mean to give us so much government! Whenever there is a conflict between what God says and what Caesar says, we must obey God rather than Caesar. We will render unto Caesar that which is Caesar's and unto God that which is God's. And, we must not permit Caesar to decide what belongs to whom.

We should flood the White House with protest letters concerning House Resolution 41 and the IRS inquiry of charitable organizations. We should also write our U.S. Senators and Representatives the same letter. But, most Christians are so busy making a buck they can't take time to protect their liberty. In fact, their lethargy is a main weapon in the arsenal of Dees as he fulfills his promise to wipe out the right wing; but those lethargic, conservative Christians will be wiped out at the same time.

Testimony at IRS Hearing
Washington, D.C.
December 6, 1978
Dr. Don Boys

Mr. Commissioner and members of the panel:

Conservative Christians are, by nature, law-abiding citizens. We believe government is from God. We teach and preach that we should obey even ridiculous laws. We teach our children to respect policemen and pray for elected officials. However, we **must** not, **can** not, and **will** not obey government if by obeying government it means we disobey God.

We believe that we must give an account to God for how we serve Him, but how can we stand before God in confidence if we disobey Him simply to have a little temporary safety? Ben Franklin said, "They that can give up essential liberty to obtain a little temporary safety deserve neither liberty or safety." We prefer liberty to safety. We have had the IRS in our pocket; now we are fighting to keep you off our back.

We will not cooperate with the IRS. It is not a matter of being stubborn. It is a matter of doing right. We have preached that we should always do right whether it is pleasing, profitable or popular, and we would be exposed as public hypocrites if we bowed to government pressure to avoid the stigma of being labled a lawbreaker.

However, if we be lawbreakers, then we are in good company. I remind you that the mother of Moses refused to obey the king and kill her son. The Egyptian midwives, likewise, disobeyed the king and refused to kill all male children born to the Israelites.

The king of Babylon tried to force 3 young Jewish men to bow to his golden image. They refused and were thrown into the furnace of fire. Much to the chagrin of the government, they came out of the furnace without the smell of smoke on their clothes and not a hair was singed.

Daniel refused to obey a new law that said no man could pray for a 30 day period, and he went into the den of lions for his courage. The law was passed just to "get" Daniel. Other governments have been known to pass laws just to "get" Christians.

Paul, Peter, James, and John likewise were lawbreakers. Peter, the apostle said, "We must obey God rather than men." We believe only God deserves unqualified obedience. We obey Him without question, whereas, we obey parents, policemen, judges, superiors, state legislatures, Congress, and the Supreme Court only as long as their commands do not conflict with God.

Concerning your proposed regulations, our school in Indianapolis is not in danger since we have more than the required percentage of blacks. In our 8 year history, I never counted blacks in our school. However, a few weeks ago during chapel, I found myself counting blacks. The IRS has, to a degree, made me a racist. Color should be irrelevant.

Our objections to the proposed regulations are numerous:

1) We find it incredible that Congress would permit a major decision like this to be made by an agency, an agency, obviously out of touch and uninformed as to the Christian school movement. I remind you that the Christian school movement is older than the Public Schools. In fact, they predate the Constitution.

2) The First Amendment forbids an agency or Congress to interfere in our ministries. If a church opens a gas station on the corner, that business should be regulated just like all other gas stations. However, our schools are as much a part of our ministry as our Sunday school, our Sunday night service and revival meetings. Either we control our ministries or we don't. The degree of control is irrelevant. Once the principle is breached, we are through. We will not justify our position to anyone before we minister to folk. If you can tell us how to run our church schools, you can tell us how to run all our churches. Evidently you do not understand that we believe all truth is God's truth. All subjects: math, English, history, science are taught from a Christian perspective, so we are religious schools and outside the bailiwick of the IRS. To those who assert that we church people think we are something special, we plead guilty. We are special. If you don't like that, change the Constitution.

3) According to the proposed regulations, you will assume we are guilty if we don't have the proper mixture of races. You should blush with shame at such a proposal. Presumptive guilt is not in keeping with our American heritage. If I should pull a gun and shoot a member of this panel while the T.V. cameras are rolling exposing the murder to a million people, I am presumed innocent until found guilty by a jury of my peers. The government will even pay for my defense. Yet, church-schools are presumed guilty of discrimination if they can't count a predetermined number of black faces in their student body!

Have you considered the possibility that a church school may not have the proper mixture because of residential patterns? There may not be blacks in close proximity to the school. Maybe blacks simply have no interest in a particular Christian school especially if the rules are strict. Further, our schools usually reflect our congregations and generally they are 98% white. We will not enroll black students in our schools simply because they are the "proper" color. They must qualify just like every other student. To do otherwise, is blatant racism.

4) To permit any **state** agency to decide guilt is irresponsible.

5) Religious convictions will not permit pastors with principle to bow to this government edict thereby forcing the issue to litigation and finally forcing them into jail. Is the U.S. government prepared to send thousands of preachers to jail for their Bible-based convictions? Let me assure you that this will be the result. We are not a bunch of red necks trying to defend an indefensible position: the hatred of another race. We are men who believe the Bible to be the Word of God and who believe in Constitutional government. We would die for either, but we will not obey government when it conflicts with God.

6) We cannot permit **any** outside force to control our church schools and dictate our internal policies. We must remain free and independent to operate superior Christian schools as a goading influence to the decaying public school system. The American people have a right to an alternative to the public schools. They must have that freedom of choice. However, if the IRS runs our schools, we will be little better than the public schools.

7) Finally, the harassment and intimidation of Churches will be a major political blunder.

In closing, I would like to make the following comments, reflecting on the testimony of others who evidently believe in coercion instead of the constitution:

1) Some critics of Christian schools who testified today such as the NAACP and the ACLU have not even tried to disguise their prejudice and hatred. I didn't think they were capable of hatred.

2) Mr. Commissioner, we should not have to spend our time and money to be here today fighting these regs. You should be trying to encourage us; not the opposite. In my 8 years in Christian education, no bureaucrat has ever called me and said: "Don, I hear that you people in Indianapolis are doing a great job helping children. What can I do to help you do a better job?" In fact, no bureaucrat, state or federal has ever done that but we in the Christian school business do hear, "do it this way or I will use the power of my office to close you down." We not only have the world, the flesh and the devil against

us; we also have hundreds of petty state and federal bureaucrats to contend with.

3) We don't owe our tax exempt status to the indulgence or kindness of the IRS but to the U.S. Constitution. Our position is: You cannot withdraw what you did not award.

4) You must understand that just because the IRS, NAACP, or ACLU makes a statement accusing Christian schools of prejudice, that does not make the statement true.

5) We believe this is a power-grab emanating from the inter-sanctum of the National Education Association to control all education. We will not be controlled by anyone.

6) We will not lie down and play dead. We will not meekly close our doors. If we go out of existence, it will not be with a whimper but a bang: letters, rallies, court battles, etc. We are prepared to fight to maintain our freedom of religion.

7) If it comes to a choice where government must choose between racial rights and religious rights, we believe religious rights must have precedence.

8) We will run our own ministries even if we lose our tax exempt status.

9) We suggest you use your clout not to interfere with and intimidate dedicated Christian people but to close down abortion mills where they slaughter babies. Evidently, you think abortion mills are legitimate because they butcher babies without regard to race, sex, color, or national origin!

10) Finally, I suggest you "deep-six" all these proposed regulations.

February 23, 1977

The Honorable James E. Carter
President, United States of America
The White House
1600 Pennsylvania Avenue
Washington, D.C. 20003

Dear Mr. President:

I am writing to express my concern over Paul Warnke whom you have recommended as Chief Negotiator for the SALT agreements, and as Director of the Arms Control and Disarmament Agency. I am sure you are aware that he is listed in the Justice Department files as a foreign agent of Communist Algeria (Registration Number 2564)! On March 14, 1976 Warnke appeared before the Senate

Budget Committee and expressed his reservations toward a strong military posture in response to questions from Senator Griffin. At that hearing he expressed his irresponsible views on the SM Tank, the ICBM, the B-1 Bomber and the Trident Submarine. He could not endorse any of these.

Mr. President, if Warnke does our negotiating we will end up with two leaky row boats armed with rusty shotguns for our national defense. I believe most Americans believe that we should be so strong militarily that the belligerent nations of the world will only want to talk with us, not fight.

Warnke has gone on record as an advocate of unilateral disarmament and has opposed the concept of the U.S. military superiority. It is incredible that you would even consider putting him in such a strategic position as this. I not only question his philosophy that could jeopardize the security of America, but I question his sense of morality. According to Congressman Lawrence P. McDonald, Mr. Warnke, "set in motion the chain of events that allowed Daniel Ellsberg to steal the Pentagon Papers."

Mr. President, I strongly urge you to withdraw your recommendation of Warnke in the best interest of this great Republic. Let's not put a fox in the hen house to guard the chickens!

Sincerely,

Donald Boys
State Representative

DB / ld

September 5, 1978

Mr. Jimmy Carter, President
United States of America
White House
1600 Pennsylvania Avenue
Washington, D.C. 20500

Dear Mr. Carter:

I write this letter as one born again Christian to another; as one elected official to another; as one concerned American to another. I know the pressure on you from all sides is fantastic, but I must make you aware of my concern and I assure you I represent millions of Americans. I don't know if the programs that I will mention are yours or your advisors, but you must accept responsibility since you have not repudiated them.

I'm concerned that we're kicking our long time friends and kissing our avowed enemies. I see you taking every opportunity to berate South Africa, Rhodesia, South Korea, Iran, Chile, Brazil, and Argentina while not saying much and doing less over the horror in Cambodia, Cuba, China, Russia and her satellite countries. Has it become fashionable to ingratiate ourselves to our enemies by castigating those nations friendly to us who have assumed an anti-Communist and pro-American posture? If an individual acted thusly to others, would he not be accused of having a death wish? Do we have a national death wish?

It is obvious that you plan to kiss off Taiwan, our long time ally, and hug Red China to your bosom. The unforgivable treatment of Chiang Ching-kuo, President of Free China, was a kick in the teeth to an old friend. It was the epitome of poor diplomacy to miss the swearing-in of Chiang, but it was made worse by Brzezinski's disgraceful bootlicking in Peking on the very day of Chiang's inauguration when Brzezinski told that gaggle of international gangsters that President Carter "is determined to join you in overcoming the remaining obstacles in the way of full normalization of our relations."

Of course you are aware that formal ties with Taiwan is one obstacle you must overcome. Then you must remove our troops stationed there, but the big obstacle is the Mutual Security Treaty of 1954 with Taiwan that must have Congressional approval if it's to be dissolved. Surely you don't think Congress is so supine that it will rubber stamp your capitulation to our enemies. I agree with Senator Goldwater that it is an impeachable offense for a President to try to abrogate a treaty without consent of Congress. I hope you don't miscalculate the mood of the Congress and the American people.

Friends are hard to come by and we should have learned that we cannot buy them. If it were possible to buy friends, we would have them all over the globe since our billions in foreign aid have been generously spread around to friends and enemies for more than 30 years.

I'm also concerned over the administration's position on Africa. As you know, most African countries are ruled by black tyrants where majority rule is a farce. But, you can't seem to get indignant over inequities in those nations. Instead, I see you wining and dining black oppressors in the White House, and showing your congeniality by hugging them as you did the President of Tanzania. Most of the black tyrants are red, and that should make them all the more persona non grata. Is this the season to court red blacks? If so, for what purpose? I personally dislike Reds of all skin color for a good reason; they want to bury me and all free people.

However, what of our treatment of the legitimate governments of South Africa and Rhodesia? We treat them like criminals. Surely, you're aware that the white governments brought civilization, railroads, telephones, telegraphs, hospitals, schools, and churches to Africa. The tyranny, bloodshed, thievery, slavery, and primitive conditions were already there.

I should think we would support these countries if only in our own self-interest. You are aware of the raw materials available in those countries; diamonds and gold from South Africa, and chrome from Rhodesia. But equally important is the fact that South Africa controls the sea lanes near the tip of Africa. As you know, much of our foreign oil supply travels that route in the giant oil tankers that cannot negotiate the Suez Canal because of their size. Are your actions calculated to turn off our lights so we can count our worthless money in the dark of a Long Cold Night?

And what of land-locked Rhodesia? Here is a brave struggling nation trying to satisfy the clamor of the busy-bodies of the world to implement a black-controlled government. They are trying to cooperate. Yet, instead of lifting our embargo and lending our moral support for these attempts, we insist that they include in their fragile plan the very communist terrorists who have publicly stated their unwillingness to work with a legitimate black government. The black leaders even demand that their terrorist guerrilla army become a part of the army of Rhodesia! The rebels do have an experienced army; experienced at butchering helpless, innocent whites and blacks. That kind of thinking indicates that more people than Dr. Bourne are snorting coke and smoking the funny stuff around the White House.

I am concerned over the persecution and prosecution of dedicated FBI men while draft dodgers and deserters go free. Did the cowards go **free** because they refused to serve their country in its distress, and are intelligence agents being **harassed** because they sought to **defend** innocent citizens from radical terrorists? Furthermore, are you willing to admit that there is any connection between the terrorists and the communists?

I am concerned that there are indications that the U.S. will soon recognize the bloody governments of Vietnam and Cuba. Have we lost all our principles? Have we forgotten the maimed bodies, orphaned children, widows, and over 50,000 flag-draped coffins that resulted from our debacle in Vietnam? Would you compound the humiliation by giving respectability to those international gangsters in Hanoi, Havana and other Red capitals? Mr. President, have we lost the ability to recognize our enemies as our enemies? I hope not.

Mr. Carter, I could go on and on for many pages expressing my concern over inflation, deficit spending, foreign aid, SALT II, defense capabilities, ERA, minimum wage, union power and corruption, national health insurance, the Humphrey-Hawkins Bill, Genocide Treaty, Panama Canal Treaties, etc.

Yes, I could go on and on, but it wouldn't do any good because you'll never see this letter. Your highly paid aides will never permit it. However, when my grandchildren ask me what I did to keep this great Republic from going down the tubes, I'll be able to tell them I spent 15 cents to make my views known. We will read this letter in secret because in a few years it will be dangerous to our health to speak or write so bluntly.

When I first heard that the Democrats might nominate a born-again Christian, I had great hopes for this nation. But those hopes were soon shattered early in your campaign when you espoused all the discredited liberal programs that were dredged from an inglorious Democratic past. I will work to defeat you, not because you're a Democrat (some of my favorite men are Democrats, like Congressman Larry McDonald from Georgia.) I will try to defeat you because your bankrupt programs will bankrupt the nation and render us helpless and make it impossible to honestly say America is "the land of the free and the home of the brave."

Yours for freedom with responsibility,

Donald Boys
State Representative

Editor
INDIANAPOLIS STAR
307 North Pennsylvania Street
Indianapolis, Indiana 46204

To the Editor:

I've served two years in the House of Representatives and it's been a great experience. I expect to be returned next year, but time and voters will decide that. It's been a demanding yet exciting time. I've made good friends on both sides of the aisle and from both extremes of the political spectrum.

One thing I learned many years ago was that you can't question a person's motives. It's difficult to know your own motives, but it's extremely dangerous and difficult to question the motives of others.

I have discovered since I've been in the House that some reporters have a very special ability to know the "thoughts and intents of the heart." Reporters and journalists have brought great joy and precious information to me by their writings. I read everything from the radical left to the radical right and many things in between. But, I have also discovered that some reporters are like many judges. They have a Messianic complex. They seem to be standing around waiting for a vacancy in the Trinity. When some of them go for a walk, they head for the lake and expect to walk on water! Maybe that's why some of them are all wet.

Last week, the **Indianapolis News** published a column by Wade Mann that insulted most members of the General Assembly. It was called, "A Renter's Defeat." It should have been called, "A Liberal's Lament." I believe in a free press. I would not want to live in a country without freedom of the press and freedom of religion. However, Mann's article makes even the bad reporters look good. He said, "the defeat of the Landlord-Tenant bill was a victory for the forces of organized greed and intellectual cowardice." Mann has a right to think the Landlord-Tenant bill might "rank as the single most important piece of legislation in the 1978 General Assembly." But, he is confused. He does not understand that it is only his opinion; an opinion not supported by the facts.

I don't question the sincerity of the sponsors of that bill. I think they were interested in helping people. But, I had sincere objections to it, and now, I find that because I voted against it, I'm something less than honest. Mann says, "such legislators, it should be stated, impeach their own intellectual capacity for public office. They ought to resign." No, Wade Mann and his type of journalist should resign.

These journalists should then run, not walk to the Secretary of State's office. And, after exposing their financial soul, they should file for office. They should run for the General Assembly, and after an arduous winning campaign, they can come to the legislature and produce such wonderful legislation they believe in. But, they don't want to run for office; they feel more qualified telling us how to vote.

Mann said, "in this basic test of legislative integrity, sixteen Republicans voted for the bill and deserve full acclaim." He then lists those Republicans who voted right, according to him. Those sixteen Republicans believed that it was the right thing to do. I think they were wrong. I have the responsibility to vote in the best interests of my district and this state.

Mann closes his tirade by saying, "the Landlord-Tenant issue then was a battle between cowardice and courage. How tragic it was that in that battle, cowardice - abetted by greed - won the final victory." To think they killed a tree to print such tripe!

Mann and the **News** owe an apology to every member of the General Assembly. We should appreciate reporters and newspapers who are fair, accurate, and balanced. But these nabobs of jittering journalism are a disgrace to their profession. We have witnessed in recent days, male and female reporters castigating legislators, questioning our motives, and presenting themselves as being wits. I think maybe they're half right!

Sincerely,

Donald Boys
State Representative

NEWS RELEASE
INDIANA HOUSE OF REPRESENTATIVES
December 9, 1977
FOR IMMEDIATE RELEASE

(Greenwood). . . State Representative Don Boys (R-Greenwood) today announced he has asked one million Christians throughout the U.S. to flood NBC with protest letters against the cancellation of Anita Bryant as co-host of the Orange Bowl Parade telecast.

Boys said, "Bryant is an active spokesman for God, family and country and is a thorn in the side of the strutting sissies who flaunt their perversion on radio, TV, magazines and in city parks."

"Liberals have proven once again they are pious hypocrites who demand free speech for liberals, but not for conservative Christians who try to be an elevating influence and make positive contributions to society. They would cut off Bryant's opportunity to discuss the issues of perversion on TV talk shows and radio shows, and the opportunity to function as a performer," he continued.

"There are still millions of Christians in America who have not swallowed the permissive liberal philosophy that anything goes as long as it is between consenting adults," Boys said.

"We still believe homosexuality is a running sore on society, but radicals would have men doing whatever feels good, as if Jesus Christ never walked on earth and told men how to live. Listening to liberals, one would think God gave us the "Ten Suggestions" instead of the "Ten Commandments" that are definite rules for human conduct," said the Indiana legislator.

Boys has written key leaders in all 50 states asking them to contact those in each state concerning his NBC protest campaign. Individuals may send protest letters to NBC, 30 Rockefeller Plaza, New York, NY 10020. He expects at least one million letters to be received by network officials in January and February.

"We are starting the New Year right. People who have never written before will protest because of a sense of anger and frustration," he predicted.

Like Bryant, Boys is anti-homosexuality, not anti-homosexual. Yet, the news media generally refers to the campaign as anti-gay, he stated. "There is nothing gay about homosexuality in my opinion," he said.

Last week Boys filed his "Right-to-Decency" bill in the 1978 session of the Indiana General Assembly. Among other things, it would make sodomy a felony again in Indiana. The Indiana legislator said he is for people, but against perversion.

"After all, God created Adam and Eve, not Adam and Steve. And I believe God knows what He's doing," he concluded.

September 19, 1977

The Honorable Otis R. Bowen, M.D.
Governor, State of Indiana
Room 206 State House
Indianapolis, Indiana 46204

Dear Governor Bowen:
I'm writing you concerning an issue that has come to my attention as I travel throughout the state. There are similar problems in Ft. Wayne, Indianapolis, Bluffton and other cities. This problem has all the ingredients of an explosive situation. I'm concerned because some of my friends and constituents are, or will be involved. However, I am more concerned over the possibility of a constitutional conflict between church and state. I can also see that men of conscience will be forced to take firm positions that will result in good men going to jail for a principle.

The state is prosecuting the Seymour Baptist Temple and Reverend Martin Jones. The church refuses to license their pre-school because they believe the state has no constitutional authority to force a church to seek a license. Some of us who avidly believe in the separation of church and state believe it is arrogant for a state to even consider such action. The state has no more authority over a church, than a church has over the state!

Please consider the following in justification of their position:

1. The Seymour church is not "just being stubborn." It is a matter of principle, a principle long held by Baptists that they will "render unto Caesar that which belongs to Caesar, and unto God that which belongs to God." Conservative Christians believe the state gets its authority from God, not God getting His authority from the state. We are supposed to be a nation under God. The state seems to have decided what belongs to God and what belongs to the state. We believe that is forbidden by the First Amendment.

2. The Seymour church already qualifies for the license. It is not a matter of their trying to put their pre-school kids in a fire trap. They could resolve this issue easily, but at the expense of their conscience.

3. Many religious leaders of various denominations are afraid of this precedent. If the state has authority to license and regulate pre-schools, the next step could be our Christian elementary and high schools. After that comes Sunday Schools, because such a plan is already being discussed by liberal do-gooders since Sunday Schools are educational and do not qualify as "worship." Their pitch is that

the constitution protects only worship. Nothing else.

4. Conservative Christians are the best friends this state has. They are people who generally obey the law, pay their taxes, pray for those in authority, give large sums of money to help others, fight wars without deserting, vote and usually are the first to light a candle rather than curse the darkness.

5. Churches with schools would not mind inspections for fire and safety. They want to comply but they refuse to ask the state for permission to carry out the legitimate ministries of pre-schools, schools, youth programs, Sunday schools, etc.

6. Children belong to their parents, not the state. And I have a suspicion that parents love their children more than a bureaucrat does. I also believe parents know what is best for their children.

7. Parents have the ultimate veto. If a school is too small, dirty, ill-equipped or understaffed, the parent simply refuses to enroll his child.

8. These ministries are not an appendage of the church, but they are an integral part of the church. They will not apply for a license for their pre-school anymore than they would apply for a license for their Sunday evening service.

9. The U.S. Supreme Court has ruled that Christians have First Amendment protection if it's a matter of **conviction,** not preference. This was decided in the Yoder case involving the Amish. It was a conviction, not a preference that Mr. Yoder's children not go to a public school. The court recognized his rights since it was his **conviction,** not a preference. I assure you that there are hundreds of ministers and thousands of laymen who hold the same conviction. Yoder went to jail for that conviction and Rev. Jones has gone on record to go to jail for that same conviction. There are one hundred pastors in Indiana willing to follow Rev. Jones to jail for a principle. Governor, is the state willing to jail one hundred pastors for their principles, principles based on the Bible and the U.S. Constitution?

10. Pursuing the Seymour case will entail fantastic expense for the state and for the church. Is the persecution of a small group of godly people a wise use of tax dollars, especially since the pastor will not capitulate? It will mean they will be forced to raise money to carry their case through the courts when they could be helping people.

Governor Bowen, I hope you and Attorney General Sendak will reconsider this action. Some of us who are friends of Rev. Jones are going to attend the next hearing in Seymour, scheduled for October 31st. I will invite other legislators to attend.

I have met with fifty-five Christian School administrators and over sixty pastors in the last few days. They are more concerned over this problem than they were over the horrendous child abuse bill of two years ago. The pastors are interested in meeting with you for thirty minutes, at your convenience, to express their concern for Rev. Jones and to try to resolve this problem in an amiable way. I am sure there are at least two hundred pastors of various denominations who want this meeting.

You have the authority to bring the full force of the state against Rev. Jones and his church, but it will only be a preview of scores of other cases. I must question the wisdom of this case. The state cannot win morally or politically, whatever the judicial decision. In closing, I remind you of the words of Horace, 65-8 B.C.: "Force without wisdom falls of its own weight."

Please be assured we are your friends and supporters. We appreciated your courageous stand on pari-mutuel and other moral issues. However, I trust you will consider our principles in this case. Awaiting your reply, I remain.

Sincerely,

Donald Boys
State Representative

DB / mr

cc: Attorney General Theodore L. Sendak
    Mr. Wayne Stanton, Dept. of Public Welfare
    Reverend Martin Jones

Boys' Statement At Freedom Rally
Indiana Coliseum
December 1, 1978
7,000 in Attendance

Ladies and Gentlemen, America has been great because she has been good. She has been free because she has been faithful. But America is becoming less faithful and consequently less free. We are not as good as we have been and we are not as great.

The Psalmist said in Psalms 119:45, *"And I will walk at liberty."* We have been walking free for over 200 years because we obeyed God's precepts. Verse 47 says, *"And I will delight myself in thy commandments, which I have loved."* Do we still love His commandments?

Can you remember back when America was really great? Can you remember—

When public schools were peaceful?

When our cities were safe?

When girls never hitched rides with strangers?

When criminals were in jail not hospitals or country clubs?

When degenerates were still in the closets not pulpits and classrooms?

When babies **were** born out of wedlock but there was shame and regret?

When a man went to the hospital for a couple of weeks if he ridiculed the flag; when he was buried if he spat on it?

When Americans traveled overseas and were respected and admired?

When we kept our national commitments to our friends?

When you could watch T.V. and never hear God's name taken in vain and not see a bedroom scene all week?

When you could afford to eat steak once a week?

When you could get a job done right for a reasonable price?

When a man had hair on his chest and bone in his back?

When teachers, policemen, and firefighters never carried picket signs?

When welfare was for the elderly, the sick, and the blind, not the young, the healthy, and the lazy?

When a man defended his country and felt it was his sacred duty?

When churches of most denominations gave a public invitation for folk to accept Christ as Lord and Savior?

Yes, we have become less faithful, and we are now less free. Woodrow Wilson said, "Liberty has never come from government . . . the history of liberty is the history of the limitations of governmental power, not the increase of it."

The more dependence upon government the less freedom we will enjoy. The state may appear to be benevolent as it reaches out a velvet hand to help, but I must remind you that a mailed fist is concealed inside that velvet glove.

The central question in this state and nation is: "Shall we have controlled citizens or controlled government?" I suggest that government growth is out of control and with that growth goes our liberty.

Ladies and Gentlemen, I remind you that liberty and control cannot be made to rhyme. Liberty and persecution cannot be made to rhyme. Liberty and license cannot be made to rhyme.

I hold in my hand an article from the **Indianapolis Star** telling of an investigation by the Chicago **Sun-Times** of the abortion mills in Illinois. It is a grisly tale of 12 women who had abortions in 4 or 5 different clinics and who received such poor treatment, they died. The murder mills were licensed, yet the license did not guarantee anything except an annual licensing fee paid to the state.

One doctor mentioned in the article also owns an abortion mill here in Indianapolis. He has a thriving business. Last year he was paid $796,000.00 by Medicaid to butcher babies at a discount price. And, his clinic is unlicensed by this state!

Now, let me see if I understand: The unlicensed abortion clinic goes about its business each day methodically butchering innocent babies and the state can't close it down while this pastor, who has dedicated his life to help people, may go to jail for refusing to permit the state to license his church pre-school! This is indicative of the moral tailspin our nation is in.

I am greatly concerned over the accelerating move in state and federal government to regulate our lives, businesses, farms and professions. Consequently, I expect to be a candidate for the U.S. Congress from the Sixth Congressional District, and I will win.

Now, I will be labeled a church candidate but that is better than being a tool of the union bosses or the radical women's groups. There are 5 clergymen in Congress now; all knee-jerk liberals. I believe we need one of US in the U.S. Congress. Don't you?

Don't be disturbed when you hear me identified as an ultra-conservative. That is like saying a man is ultra-honest or ultra-kind. I used to think I was a political moderate, but in recent years, the left has moved so far left it makes us appear far right. Now, if we are right does that not make the others wrong?

If they mean by ultra-conservative that I will demand a strong national defense against international communism, I plead guilty; or if they mean I want a government of laws and not the whim of bureaucrats, I plead guilty; if they mean spending only what is necessary and what is available, I plead guilty; if they mean welfare only for the deserving and jail for the thieves, I plead guilty; if they mean a complete restructuring of HEW and the IRS to where they are responsible, competent and accountable then I plead guilty.

I plead guilty to believing that preachers should not be in jail while killers and rapists stalk the streets. I plead guilty to believing that slobbering judges who tap the criminal on the wrist and stab the law abiding citizens in the back should be removed from the bench.

I plead guilty to believing that we need more conservative Christians in public office, for Christians should be the most caring, concerned, consistent, and competent people.

But, I cannot win a seat in Congress without your help. I will announce in January only if I am convinced that I have the support needed to sustain such an arduous effort. If you believe in my candidacy, take the 3 x 5 card and give me your name, address and phone number. Write on the card, "money and work." I expect every person I know to help in some way to send one of US to Congress.

My political philosophy can be succinctly framed in the words of Abraham Lincoln: "You cannot bring about prosperity by discouraging thrift; you cannot strengthen the weak by weakening the strong; you cannot further the brotherhood of man by encouraging class hatred. You cannot help the poor by destroying the rich; you cannot keep out of trouble by spending more than you earn; you cannot build character and courage by taking away man's initiative and independence; you cannot help men permanently by doing for them what they could and should do for themselves."

And, finally, as a Christian American I recommend the words of President John Kennedy that he plagiarized from Calvin Coolidge, "Ask not what your country can do for you, but what you can do for your country."

Mike, Christy and Ryan Boys

EPILOGUE

Well, I hope you now understand why I say, "Liberals are pulling on a rope of sand." But it is not enough to point out their error and to teach conservative ideology. We must have Christian people in public office. You must get informed and then involved in every level of government. But first, some guidelines.

Should you send a person to the state legislature or Congress because he is a "good ol' boy" who will play political games with the party machine, or should you help elect a person who will not "go along in order to get along?" Surely we don't want a representative who "pulls on a rope of sand." Why not send the best?

Some naive and uninformed people say, "Republicans are the good guys and the Democrats are the bad guys." It is also said by some that the Democrats are the good guys in white hats who really care for people, and the Republicans are the bad guys in black hats. I'm embarrassed for such people, because only fools or political bigots talk that way. Mental midgets with brains the size of pears and mouths the size of pineapples espouse that kind of philosophy. It is un-American, unkind and untrue.

There are good, qualified people in all political parties. I must frankly admit that there are far more conservatives in the Republican Party than in the Democrat Party. There are also some knee-jerk liberals that wear the Republican label; liberals who should be sent back where they came from. The party officials will scream "treason" at such unorthodox talk. But, my question to them is, "Are you telling me that we should elect a person to office even if he is an immoral, dishonest, weak-kneed incompetent; as long as he is a member of the 'right' party?" I suggest that kind of nonthinking is one reason for the mess in Washington and in most state capitols.

The voters should investigate each candidate and elect the one who will best represent the views of the electorate. I want a man representing me in Washington and the State House who has hair on his chest, bone in his back, something between his ears besides a hat, and empathy in his heart for all kinds of people (without being a syrupy sentimentalist who wants the government to do everything for people except tie their shoes each day.)

We must elect Christian statesmen who look toward the next generation, not the next election. I'm afraid most officials are so busy running for the next election they don't take time to think of the PRESENT generation they are supposed to be representing.

Before each politician votes, I'm sure most of them ask, "How will this be perceived back in my district?" Such men are not statesmen. Other men raise a moist finger to the air to catch the prevailing political wind, and vote that way. These are not statesmen. Others will vacillate to the left and to the right depending on where the pressure is coming from. They try to be a friend of all and a foe of none. They run with the hare and hunt with the hounds. They try to be all things to all men and end up being nothing - except politicians.

Politicians use government funds to buy votes from the welfare crowd when they promise more generous benefits, less stringent qualifications, more people covered and no prosecution for thieves. They are not statesmen.

Politicians also buy the public employees' vote by promising collective bargaining, right to strike, and generous benefits. They even support the public employees when they strike against the public and demand that "no reprisals" be a part of the settlement. These are hardly statesmen. They are, rather, accessories to the crime of arson when firemen set fires and watch them burn. They are accessories to crime as teachers walk picket lines leaving the classrooms empty. They are accessories to crime as policemen become bums and leave a city unprotected at the mercy of felons. When a city is beaten to its knees by a public employee union, the politicians must be held accountable for their crassness in buying support by giving irresponsible union bosses power over a city that the taxpayer does not have. We need a statesman who will "bell the public union cat."

If a private citizen sells his vote to a candidate at the polls, both can be and should be prosecuted, but a U.S. Senator can sell his soul and vote for the Panama Canal Treaties against the overwhelming desires of his constituents, and receive political goodies from the White House! It is ironic and incredible that the President uses taxpayer's money to buy votes for the treaties that will be counterproductive to U.S. taxpayers. Now we know where the TV program "Let's Make a Deal" came from. Not statesmenlike activities, is it? No, just politics as usual.

Is it any surprise that politicians are held in such low esteem by the American people?

Members of Congress circumvent the law forbidding the hiring of relatives by agreeing to hire each other's relatives. This is their contribution to full employment in the Halls of Congress. Very thoughtful, those politicians.

Statesmen believe that as public officials, they should be discrete, honest, industrious, and moral. Politicians don't. Politicians believe that if a man is a drunk, it is his personal business as long as he doesn't stagger in the legislative halls. Statesmen believe such men should resign from office until they win their battle with the bottle.

Politicians believe their morals, or lack of them, is a private affair even to the extent of sexual aberration. Statesmen, without being self-rightous, believe officeholders should not offend the voters with irresponsible, immature, and immoral behavior.

It is politicians, not statesmen, who push and shove their way to the public trough where they grunt, snort, and root their way to the top. Many would be failures if they had to compete in private enterprise, however, they will be very successful in the field of politics where they can buy votes with promises. They learn quickly that politics is as Aristotle said, "The art of the possible," where you "go along in order to get along." That translates "you scratch my back and I'll scratch yours." The taxpayer doesn't get his back scratched, only his pocket picked.

Christian statesmen are not in office to see what they can get, but what they can give. They put into practice the words of Calvin Coolidge: "Ask not what your country can do for you, but what you can do for your country." Not many authentic card-carrying statesmen around, are there? We Christian conservatives should get involved in sending statesmen to Congress and the state legislatures.

Daniel Webster said, "What ever makes a man a good Christian also makes him a good citizen." Webster was right.

Raymond Moley, who was an author, teacher, and advisor to four presidents said, "Politics lays a heavy hand on every circumstance of our lives. It can measurably tell us what job we may have, and what we may get for our labors. It takes our children and decrees what they should be taught. It can take our youth and destroy them in war. It can enter our dwelling and seize our private effects. If we go on as we have, it will regiment our lives from conception to dissolution. Even our quiet graves are made to specifications drawn by a bureaucrat. We must master politics or be mastered by those who do."

Christians must master politics or be mastered by those who do. We must remember to keep our priorities straight; but for a hundred years, government has had no place in our lives. We have justified our lack of involvement by being "too busy" or "everyone in government is a crook" or, "I'm a citizen of another country. I'm only passing through." So we decided to leave government to "them." And, "them" translates: liberals. We have a mess in Washington and most state capitols because Christians have been too lazy, too uninformed, too lethargic, and too warped to get involved.

Many church members think that genuine Christians should not run for political office or even help a good candidate get elected. They are wrong, dead wrong. These folk would tell us that God set up government, but He then said, "I don't want my people to get involved." What folly. Christians should be running government at every level from school boards to state legislatures to Congress. I believe we should have a born-again Christian even in the White House!

The most effective politicians should be Christian politicians. No one should be more kind, open, concerned, fair, consistent, honest, and industrious than born again Christians.

A cursory look at the Old Testament will validate God's people working in government. Joseph, although a foreigner in Egypt, was chosen Prime Minister of that great Empire. He didn't sit around and say, "I can't do much since I'm a fundamentalist. There's too much against me." He became the number two man in the Egyptian government, yet he was a type of Christ. Most Christians think that being a type of Christ was a full-time job, but Joseph went to work each day as a working politician, and he found that did not conflict with being a type of Christ.

If Joseph had been like many Christians today, he would have sat in the shadows of the pyramids, shaking his head at how wicked Pharaoh was and how corrupt the government was and what a hard time God's people were having. He decided that he would not cry about corrupt government or complain about it, but he would do something about it. And he did.

Most Bible readers think that the Judges of Israel were involved in spiritual work when the very word "judge" is a political term. They were spiritual leaders, but they were working politicians. Some good, some bad. Just like today.

Of course, the Hebrew Kings were working politicians, although most Christians think David sat all day by the riverside, singing the psalms as he thumbed his harp til he raised blisters on his fingers. But David went to the palace each day to run a government, and like all politicians, he had his strengths and his weaknesses.

What of Shadrach, Meshach, and Abednego in the Babylonian empire? They were brought as captives from Jerusalem by King Nebuchadnezzar along with the spoils of battle. The young Jews were trained to be leaders in the foreign government of Babylon. They became leaders and a fantastic testimony to their God when they refused to obey an edict of the king that would have resulted in their disobedience to God. They went to work each day as working politicians.

The prophet Daniel walked with God, yet was also a top political leader in Babylon. He was one of the godliest men in the Bible, yet he was a politician! He also refused to obey the king when to do so would violate his scripture-based convictions. So he was a politician with character. Too many politicians are simply characters.

Ninety percent of the Christians talk about good government, but don't do anything. They are good at identifying the problem, but not good at working out the solution. The fact is, lazy Christians **ARE** the problem! Thank God they are also the solution. There are over 50 million Bible-oriented Christians in America, with other millions in the old-line denominations.

We Christians could wield enough clout to affect a change in any state or federal election; eliminate immoral garbage from TV and movies; clean out the pornographers, adult book stores, massage parlors, and prostitutes in most cities; demand quality education in public schools and get it; pass a Proposition 13 in all 50 states; and generally clean out of government the big spenders, drunks, softies on crime, bleeding hearts, do-gooders, busy-bodies, junketeers, and all politicians who are in government to pad their pockets and promote their own personalities. Yes, we Christians have clout if we would only use it. But, we are so busy going to church, teaching Sunday School, tithing, and visiting, that we either think that excuses us from being a good citizen, or, we just don't have time. Wrong again. That kind of non-thinking indicates some Christians are "pulling on a rope of sand."

Most Christians have never given a dollar to get a good conservative elected. They have never handed out any campaign literature for a good man. They have never knocked on a door on behalf of a good candidate. They are quick to complain, but not quick to campaign. Much talk, but no walk. The most they have done is vote; on occasion. That describes me until a few years ago.

I thought I was a good citizen. I had never been in jail. I obeyed the law. I started six or seven churches; helped start 26 Christian schools; preached revivals around America; preached every week on TV; preached every day on radio; delivered a conservative news commentary on TV each week; yet I was not a good citizen and neither are you unless you're involved in government, or helping others get involved. However, we must keep in mind Psalm 118:9: *"It is better to trust in the Lord than to put confidence in princes."*

Churches cannot get involved in politics, but individual Christians can and should be involved. The liberal crowd implies that we Christians are second class citizens, but we are first class citizens with all the rights and privileges anyone else has.

The liberals in my state who have more brass than brains have said that my being in government is a threat to the separation of church and state. Yet, the five clergymen sitting in Congress are no threat to sepration of church and state. Could it be because they are all knee-jerk liberals? Let's see if I understand: a conservative clergyman in government is a threat to our Constitution, yet liberal clergymen are not a threat! That proves once again that liberals are not the brightest people in the world. I believe reading the **New York Times** has a tendency to rot the brain.

Many of our churches and church ministries are having trouble and many pastors have become active and informed. They have jumped into the battle as they hold impressive rallies for God and Country; as they March for Morality; as they write poignant prose in defense of liberty; as they stand up to the enemy in televised debate and clearly articulate the cause of freedom and the importance of personal Bible convictions over the arbitrary edicts of the state; as they clearly delineate between the legitimate authority of the state and the constitutionally protected rights of the churches - BUT WHERE WERE THEY ON ELECTION DAY? Are these same good pastors too spiritual to help a Christian candidate get elected? Can they not see the wisdom of surrendering some of their bus workers for a couple Saturdays to help a candidate? The day will soon arrive when they won't have a bus ministry unless sympathetic men are in office. Have you pastors not learned that you can preach, march, write, and debate but the bottom line is: our case must be heard in Congress and the state houses and it won't be heard there unless we put Christian men and women in office.

I do not advocate a church taking political sides unless it is a moral and Biblical issue like booze, gambling, sodomy, prostitution and similar issues. But pastors can take a couple of days and walk a precinct for a Christian conservative who has to run against the opposition of the union bosses, perverts and radical women's groups. The preacher's example will be an inducement for laymen to also get involved. Face it pastors, we will continue to have major problems that will require more and more time and money to fight in court and we will face liberal judges who have no heart for our cause and will often be antagonistic to that cause. The answer to our problems is to put Christians in office running the nation as God planned from the beginning; from local school boards to the halls of Congress.

It is time for Christians to get informed, stay informed, and to inform others regarding good government. It is time to write letters to the newspapers and sign petitions for conservative-Christian causes. It is time to stop whining and start to work. It is time to pick a candidate and help him throw the opportunists out of office. It is time to realize that to be a good Christian means to be a good citizen.

WOULD YOU LIKE TO START A CHRISTIAN SCHOOL IN YOUR CHURCH?

Don Boys is an educational consultant to numerous Christian schools and is also available to those churches who desire to start a school. Success for a new Christian school is not automatic. A Christian school is born through people with faith and a vision, but also requires professional know-how to become firmly established to grow and to succeed. Start today. Most Christian schools start small; many with as few as twenty-five. If you have a need, why not turn to a professional for professional help? It doesn't cost, it pays. Boys specializes in personalized curriculum. Return the coupon.

A TIME TO LAUGH
by Don Boys

The Best Collection of Riotous Jokes,
Limericks, Puns, Tombstone Humor
and One-Liners
for Public Speakers, Preachers, Politicians,
Toastmasters and Those Folks Who Enjoy
Belly-bouncing Good Clean Fun.

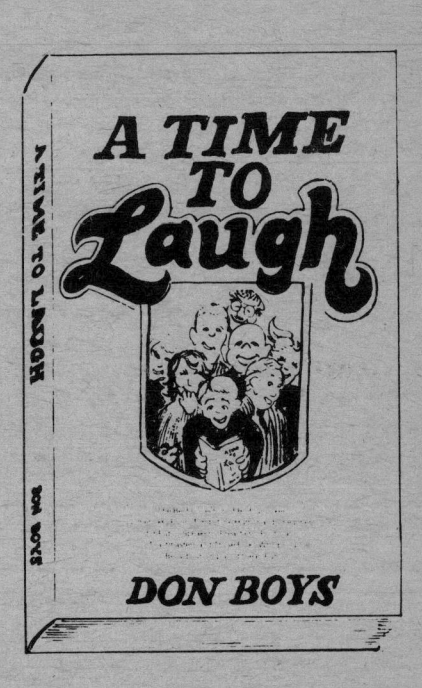

Please send me the following order — Check enclosed.

Name _____

Address _____

City _____

Send me_____copies of the book **A Time to Laugh** at $2.50 **per copy** $_____

Add 10% to total bill for shipping & handling (maximum $10.00) $_____

                                                Total order $_____

Send order and check to:

Goodhope Press, Inc.
P. O. Box 27145
Indianapolis, IN 46227

DO YOUR STUDENTS KNOW THE ANSWERS TO THE MAJOR ISSUES OF OUR DAY? THEY WILL IF YOU USE —

TRUTHPAC series —

ISSUES AND ANSWERS

by Dr. Don Boys

- Used by over 200 Christian schools the first year!
- A re-write of **Liberalism: A Rope of Sand** (now in its third printing in 12 months — seen on major T.V. stations).
- A series of 8 Truthpacs and 2 Score Keys.
- Used in traditional, cluster or individualized schools. Makes students think — stimulates discussion and debates.
- Series deals with — gay rights, ERA, abortion, welfare, capitol punishment, public employee strikes, reverse discrimination, religious freedom, free enterprise.
- Written from a Bible perspective; gives answers to hottest problems facing the free world.
- For use in 10, 11, or 12 grades — many schools require the course for graduation.
- 5-page paper required in each Truthpac.

- Comments by leading Christians:
  Dr. John R. Rice ". . . grateful for your strong stand and your sensible arguments . . . will do great good."
  Dr. Greg Dixon ". . . one of the finest available . . . leaves great impact upon the reader."
  Dr. John Rawlings ". . . is a dynamic pungent message for the heart of America."

Please send me the following order — Check enclosed.

Name _____ Phone (___) _____
Address _____
City _____ State _____ Zip _____

Send me _____ copies of each of the 8 Truthpacs at $1.25 **per copy** $ _____

Send me _____ copies of the 2 score keys at $1.25 **per copy** $ _____

Send me _____ copies of the book **Liberalism: A Rope of Sand** $4.95 $ _____

Add 10% to total bill for shipping & handling—(maximum $10.00) + _____

                                    Total order $ _____

Send order and check to:
Goodhope Press, Inc.
P. O. Box 27115
Indianapolis, IN 46227

FINALLY—WHAT MANY CHRISTIANS HAVE BEEN WAITING FOR— A HEALTH BOOK FROM THE CHRISTIAN PERSPECTIVE!!

YOUR HEALTH:

**How to Feel Better
Look Younger
Live Longer**

by Dr. Don Boys

Some facts about this exciting new book:

- Cloth bound and paperback — over 200 pages.
- The author deals with **total** health: physical, mental, social, financial and spiritual.
- Subjects dealt with in detail: food, vitamins, exercise, drug abuse, tobacco, alcohol, marijuana, peer pressure, mental attitude, salvation, service, friendships, dating, venereal disease, marriage, spiritual authority, major organs, skin, hair, etc.
- No samples will be sent since the author has established himself with his other books as to quality and fundamental position.
- The book's premise is: The body is the Temple of the Holy Spirit . . . It belongs to God. Nothing must be done to harm it.

Every State Requires Health to be Taught in High School — Why Not Use the Only Christian Text?

Please send me the following order — Check enclosed.

Name _____ Phone (_____) _____

Address _____

City _____ State _____ Zip _____

_____ Copies of **YOUR HEALTH** — Cloth bound at $7.95 $_____

_____ Copies of **YOUR HEALTH** — Paperback at $4.95 $_____

Add 10% to total bill for shipping & handling—(maximum $10.00) $_____

                                                    Total $_____

Send order and check to:

    Goodhope Press, Inc.
    P. O. Box 27115
    Indianapolis, IN 46227

Exciting Cassette Tapes by Dr. Don Boys

No.	Titles	Price
101	"The Slimepit of Children's Liberation" or "What's Really Behind the International Year of the Child?" (side one) "Gay Rights Debate" (side two)	$3.50
102	"Debate on Reverse Discrimination"	3.50
103	"A Matter of Freedom"	3.50
104	"Must Christians Always Obey the Law?"	3.50
105	"Should Christians Be in Politics?"	3.50
106	"Number One Problem of Fundamentalism" (side one) "The Question of Dying" (side two)	3.50
107	"How to Be Happy Though Married" (side one) "The Leper, the Prophet and a Cold Swim" (side two)	3.50
108	"Saul, Samuel and the Witch" (side one) "The Two Prophets" (side two)	3.50
109	"Three Soldiers at Calvary" (side one) "The Great Question" (side two)	3.50
110	"Three Preachers in the Fire" (side one) "Paul's Heart" (side two)	3.50
111	"What to Do When Government Visits" (IRS, Welfare, Health, Fire, Dept. of Labor etc.) (side one) "Keys to Success and Happiness" (side two)	3.50
112	"Professional Training Sessions" (set of three—full set only) 1. How to Control Children at Home and School 2. Spiritual Authority 3. Management of Church and School 4. How to Start a Christian School 5. How to Raise Money and Recruit Students 6. Promoting the Christian School	25.00

(Coupon on next page)

SPECIAL #1 All tapes, a $63.50 value only $45.00.
SPECIAL #2 Any 10 tapes (excepting No. 112), a $35.00 value—only $20.00.
SPECIAL #3 Any 5 tapes (excepting No. 112), a $17.50 value—only $12.00.
113 Extra Special tape — "Public Education: A Poisoned Pot"
"A Time to Fight"   5.00

Name_____

Address_____

City_____ State_____ Zip_____

Send _____ copies of *Liberalism: A Rope of Sand* at $4.95 per copy. Check enclosed.

Send me _____ cassette tapes _____
         (quantity)   (numbers or "SPECIAL")
_____ at _____. Total amount of tapes
 number)   (price)
$_____. Enclose check.

I am interested in a personalized curriculum for an existing Christian school. _____

I am interested in starting a Christian school. Send information. _____

Make all checks to:
    Dr. Don Boys
    P. O. Box 27115
    Indianapolis, Indiana 46227

Add 10% to order for shipping & handling—$10.00 maximum.